# Coloring Fun:

# Twisted Knots!

# G.O. Molloy

Coloring Fun: Twisted Knots!

Published by
G.O. Molloy

ISBN-13: 978-1517178857
ISBN-10: 1517178851

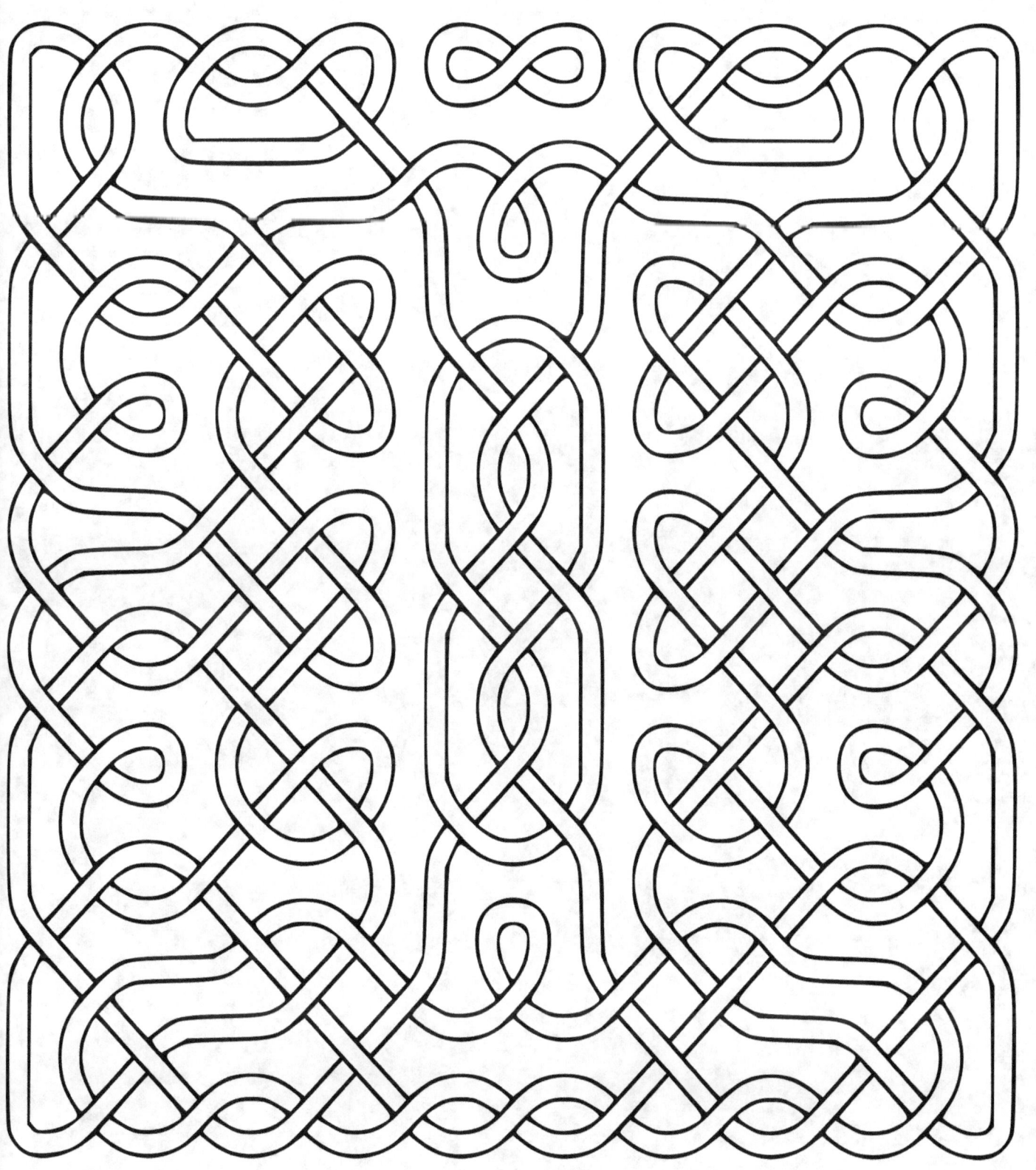

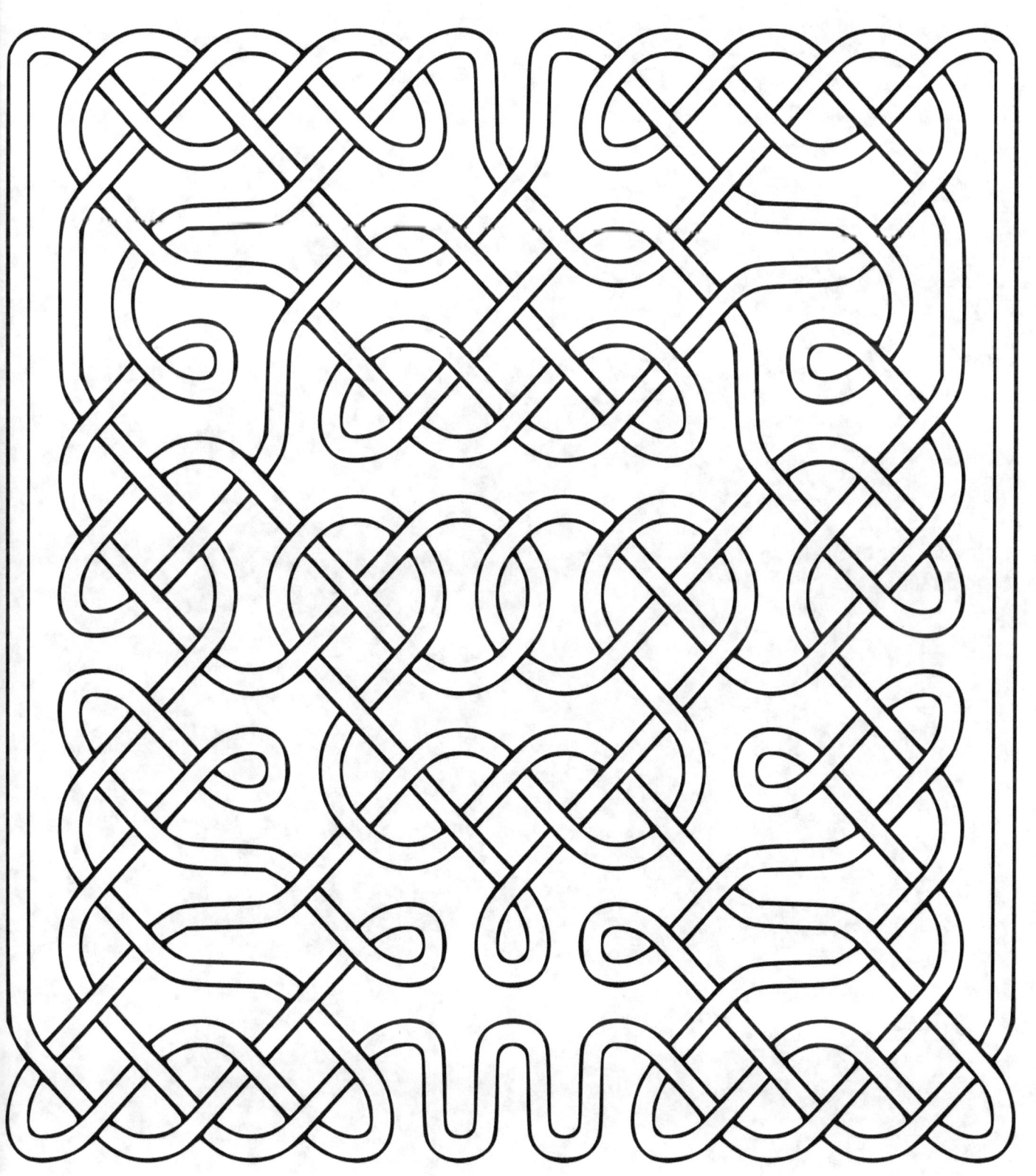

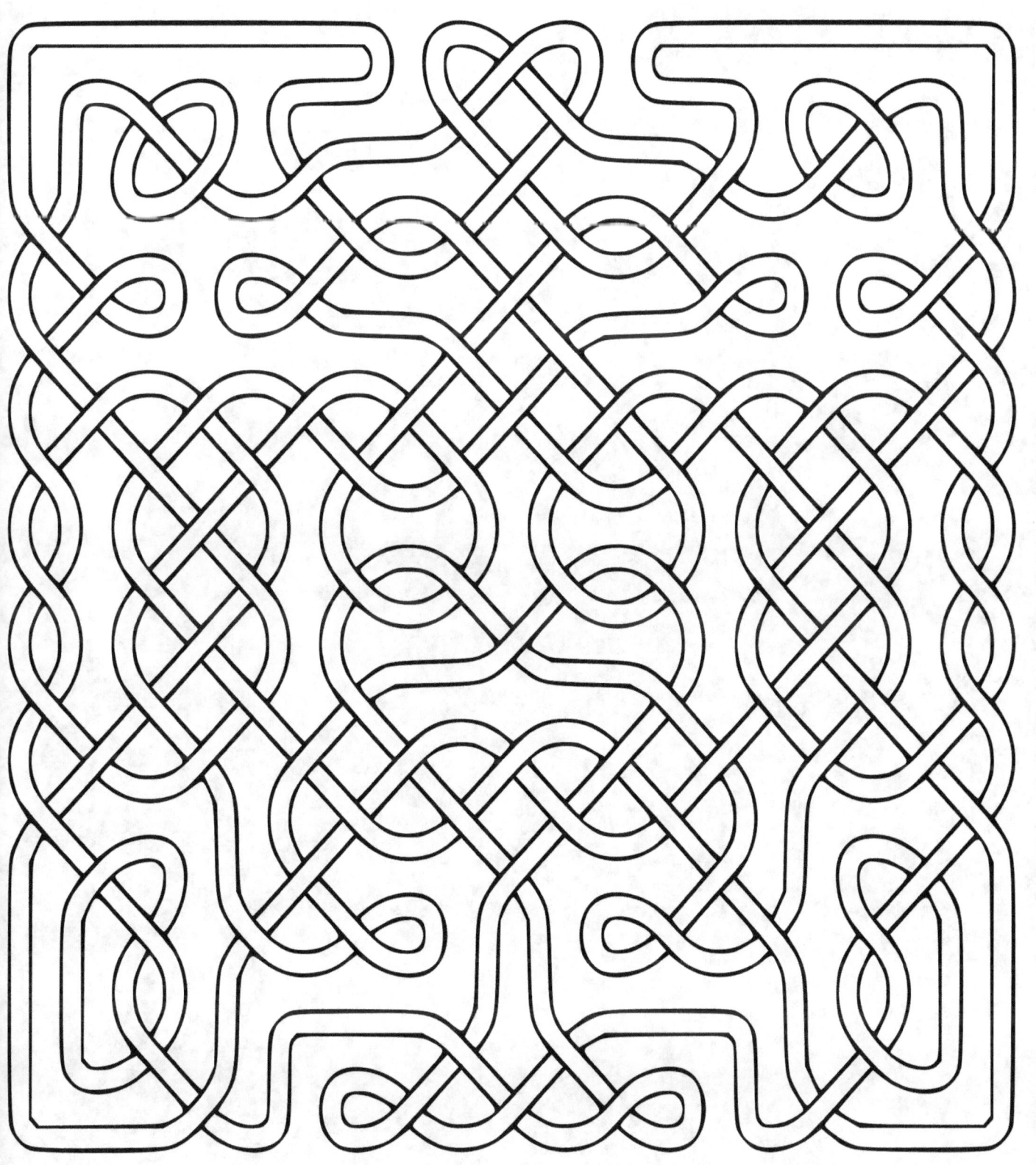

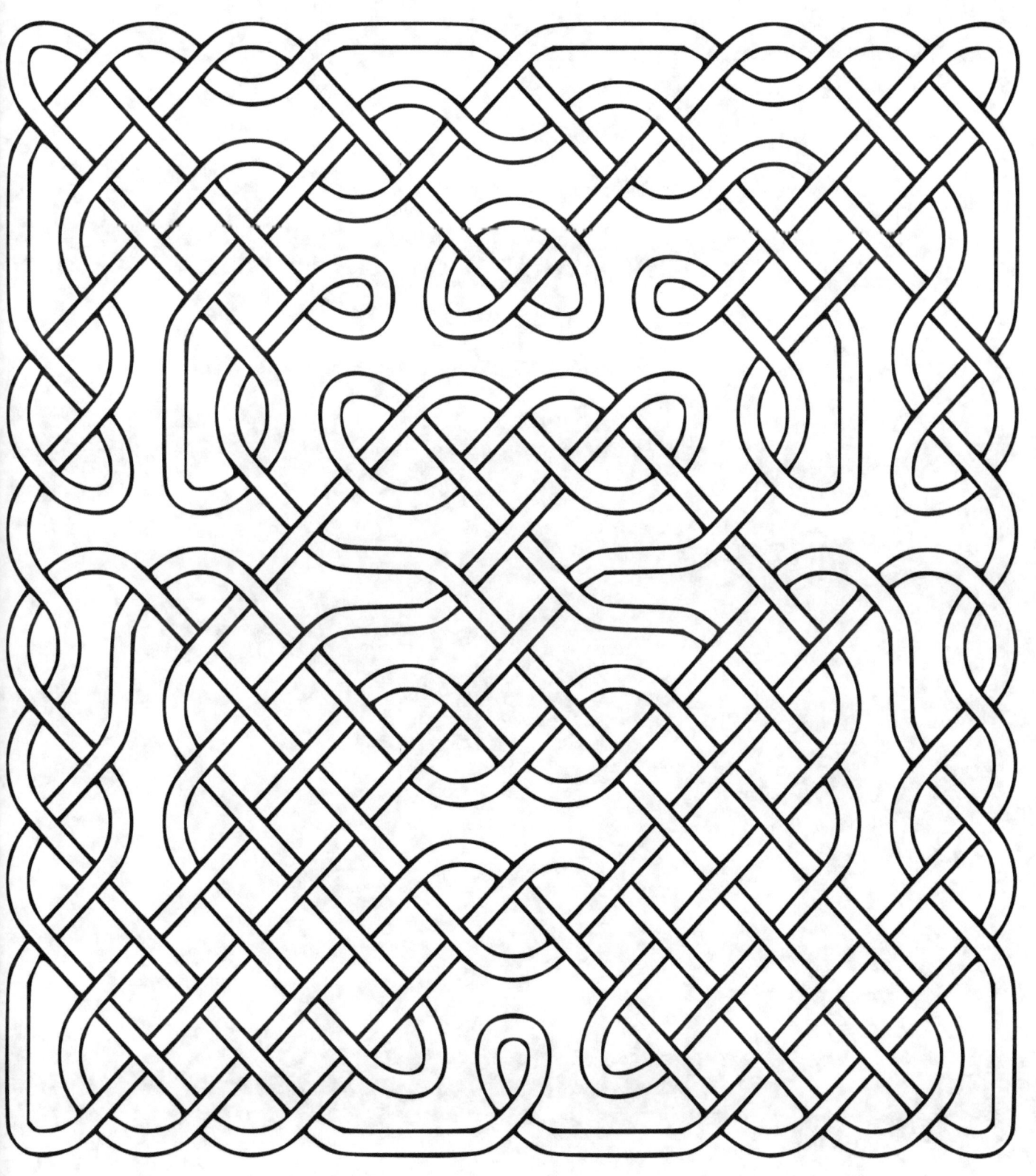

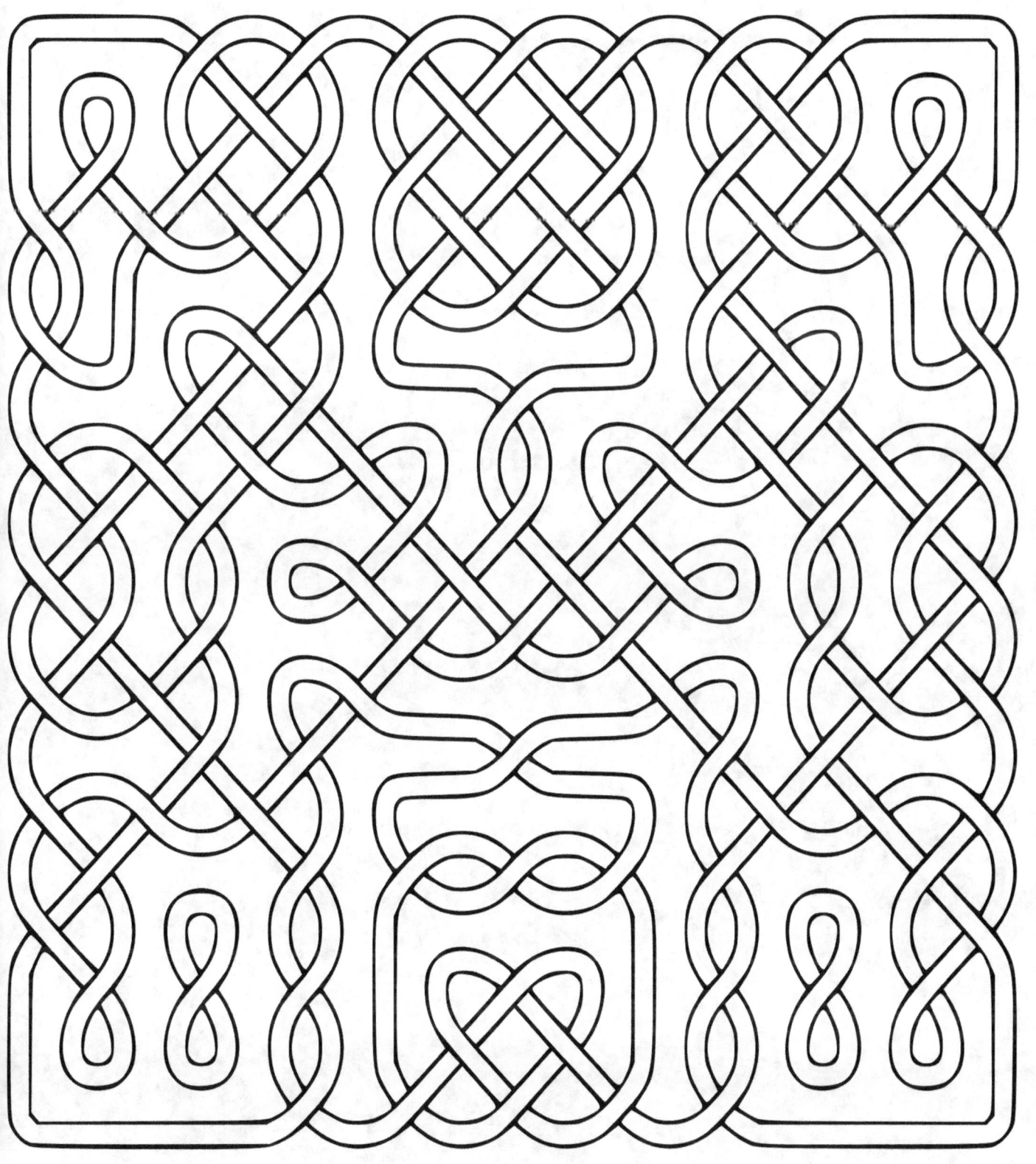

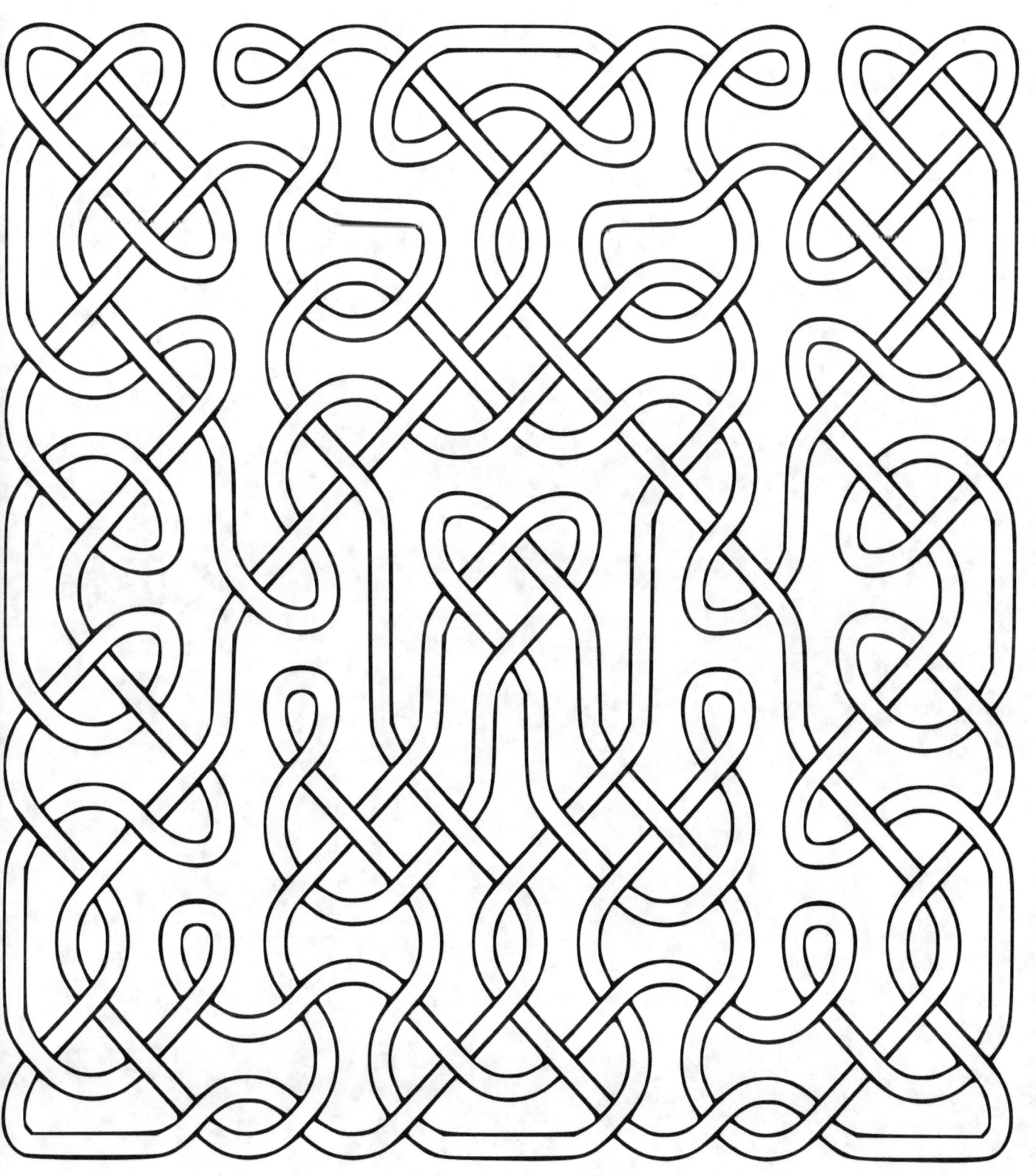

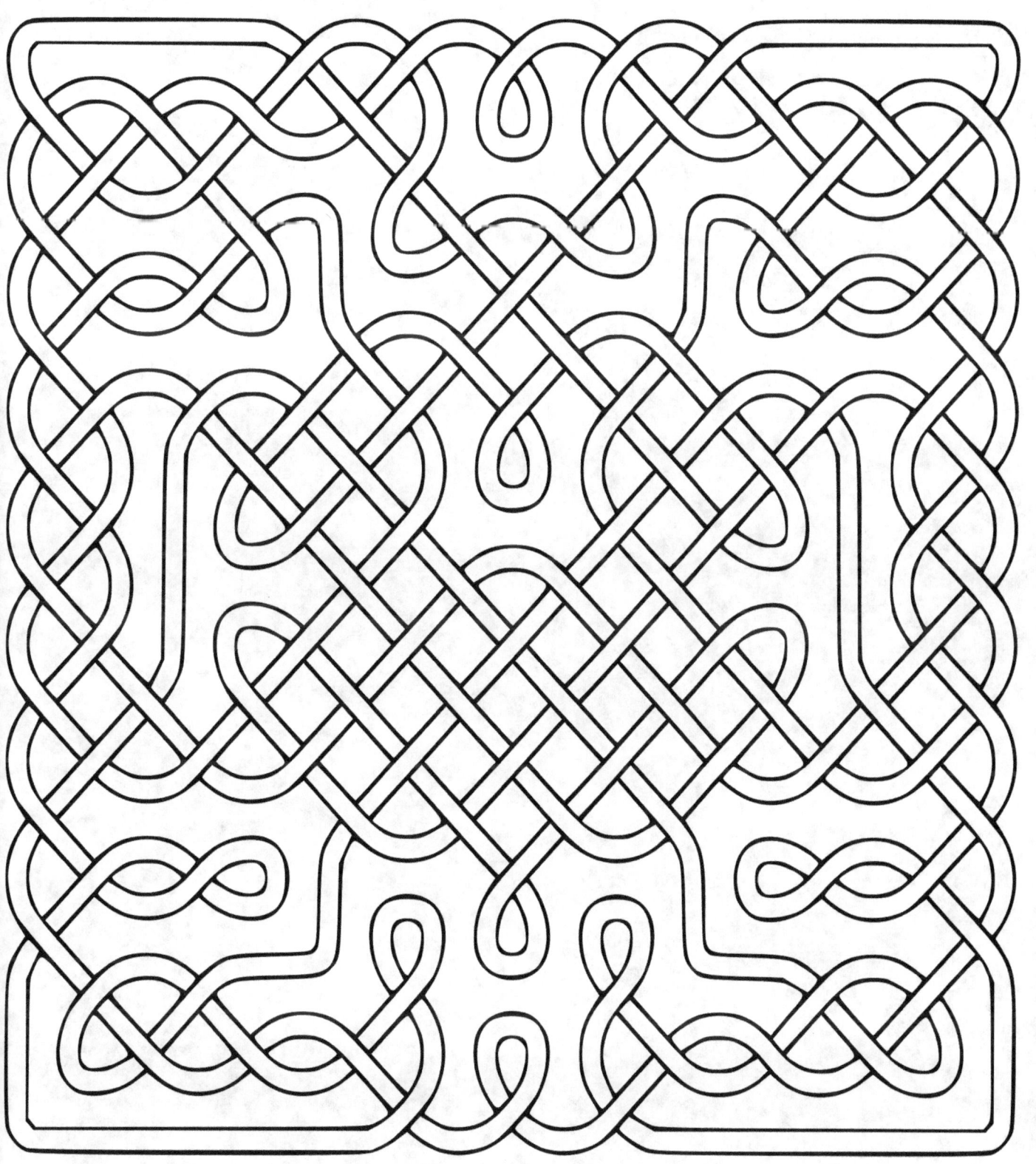

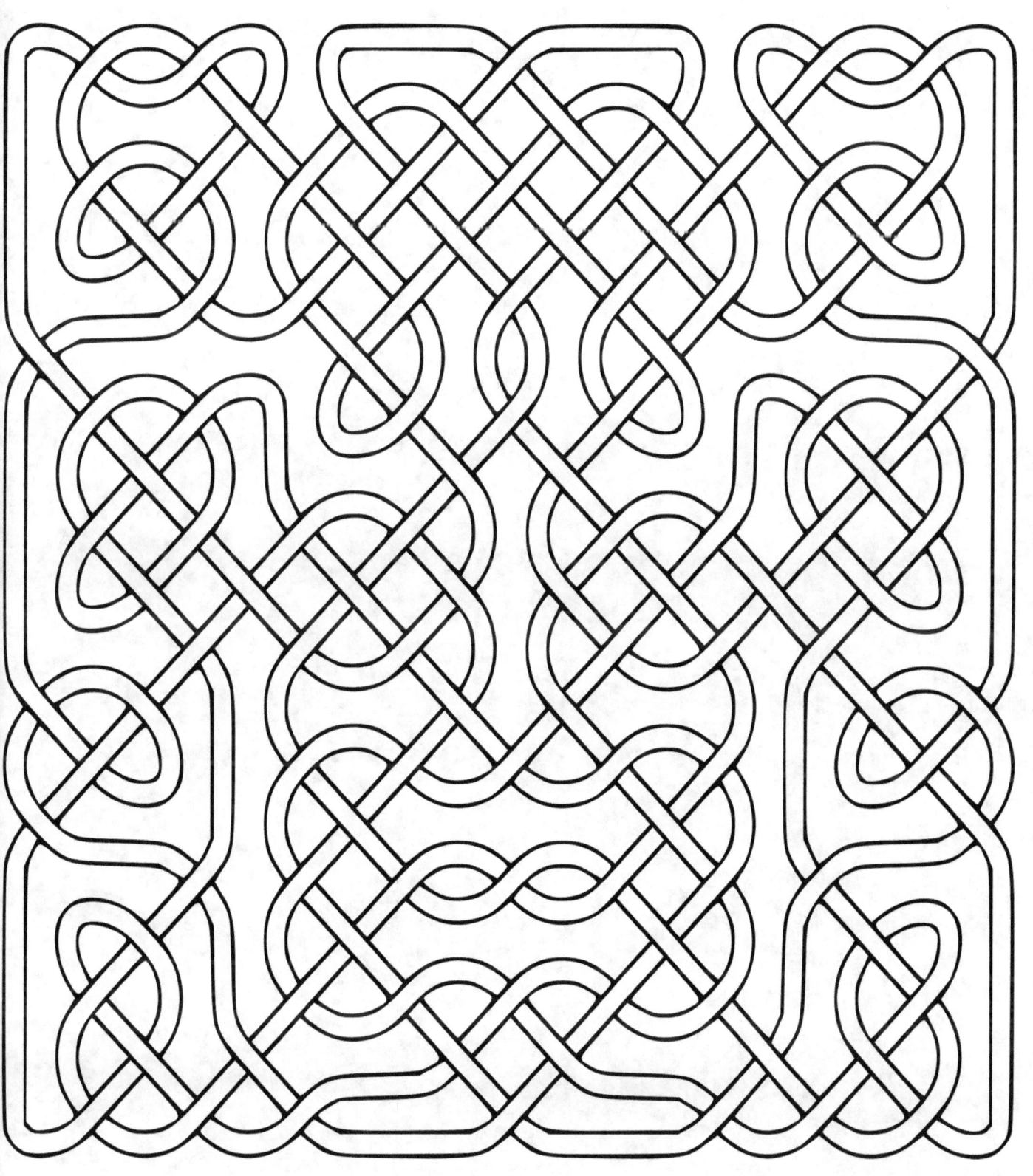

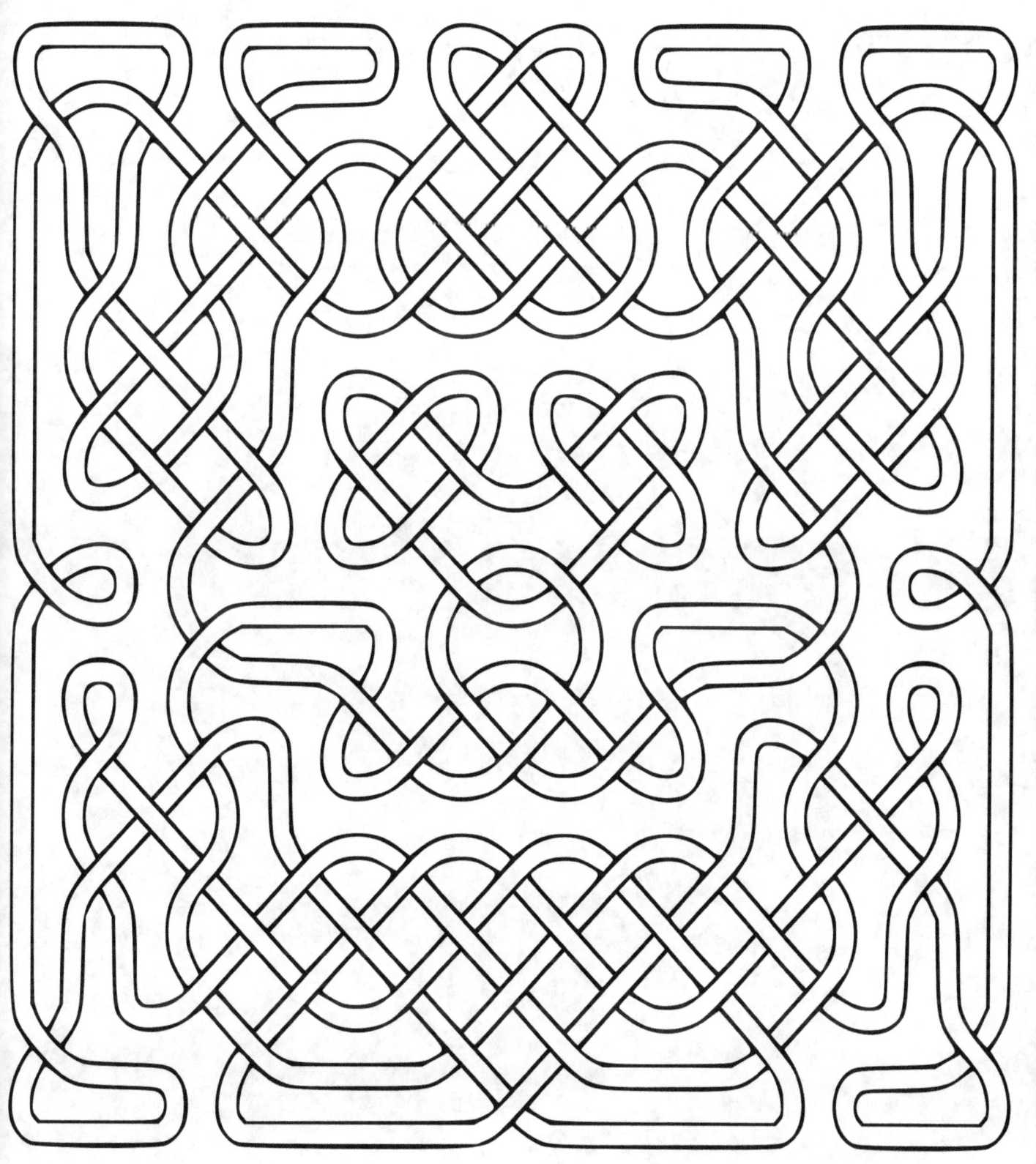

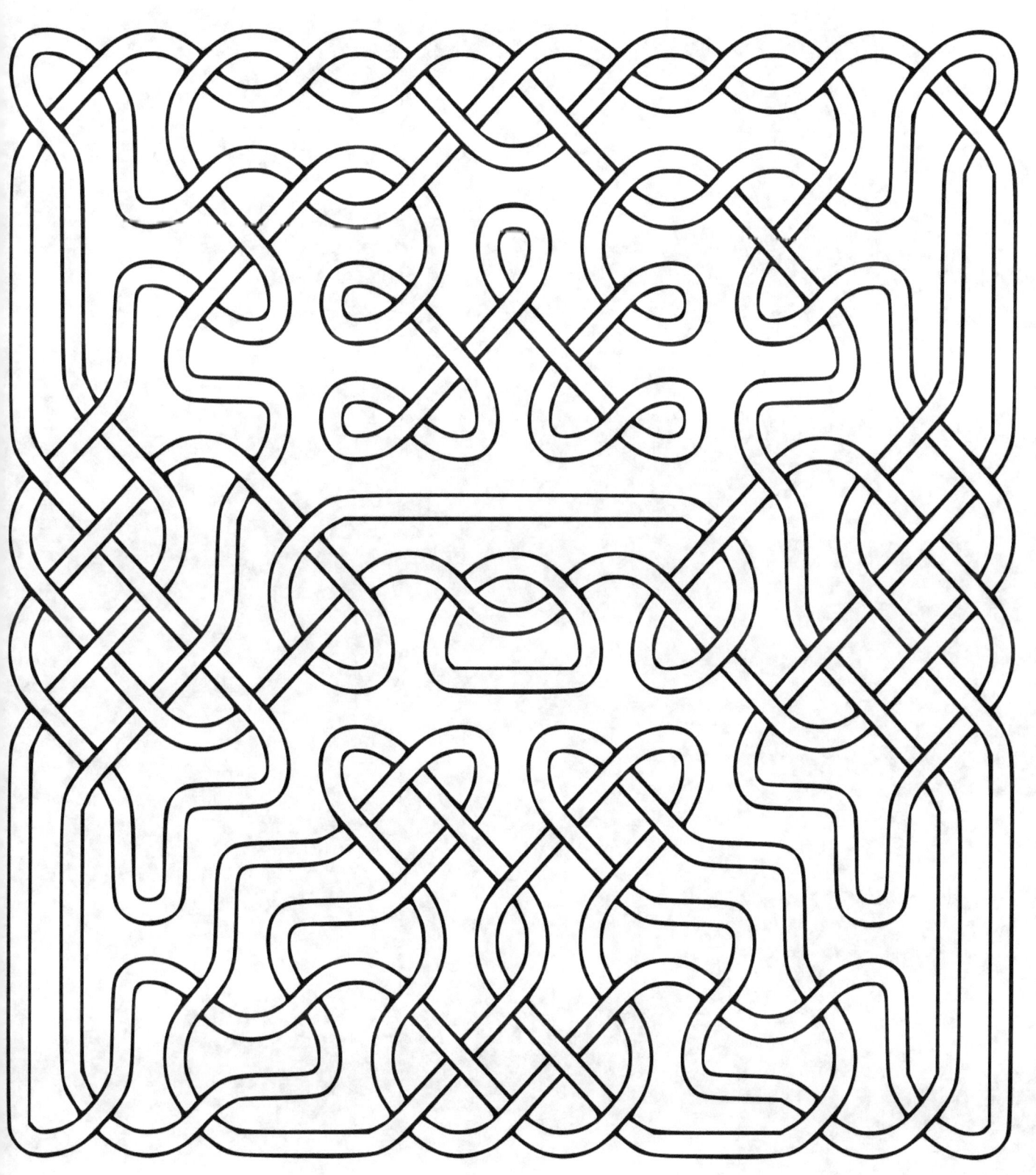

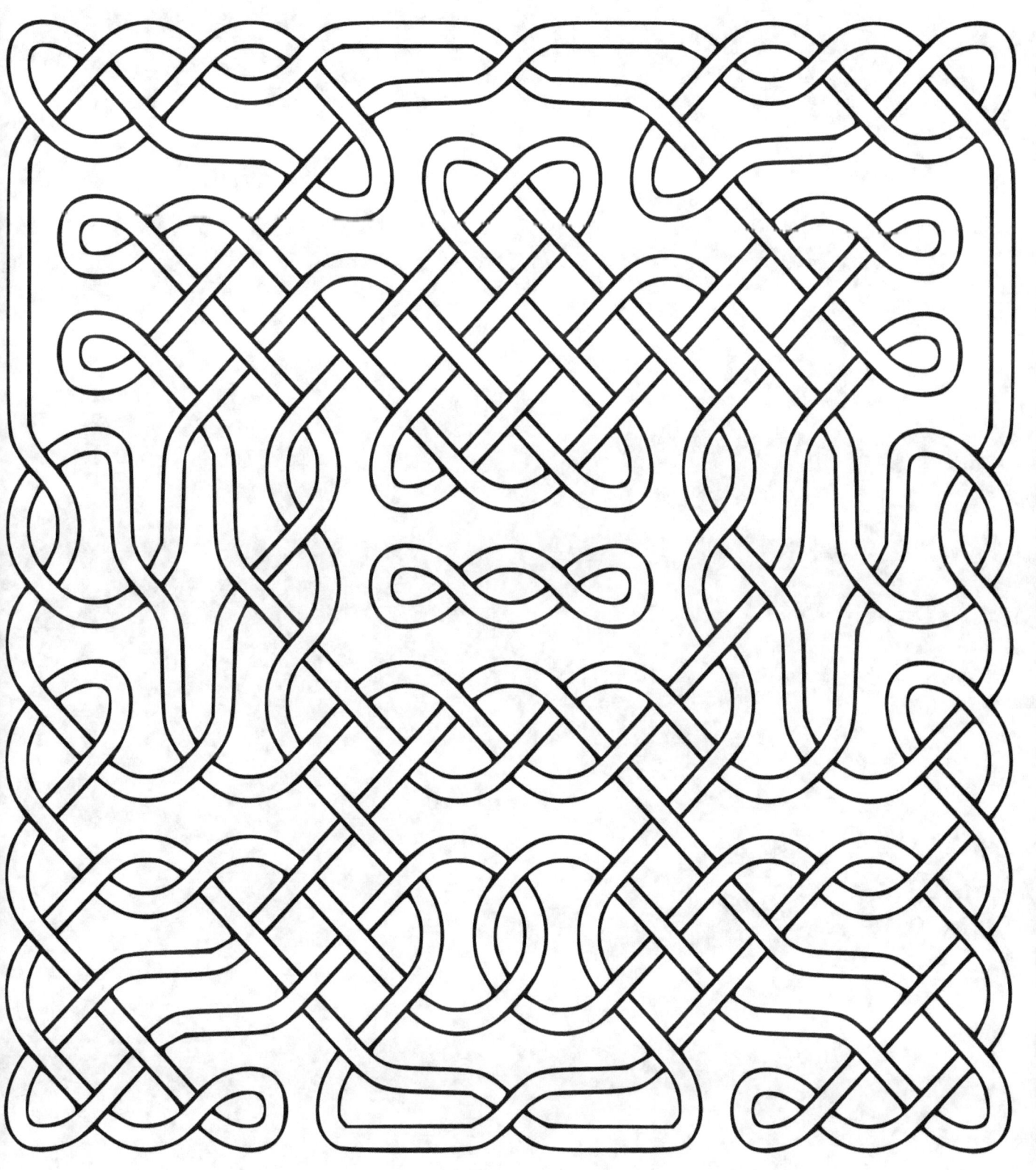

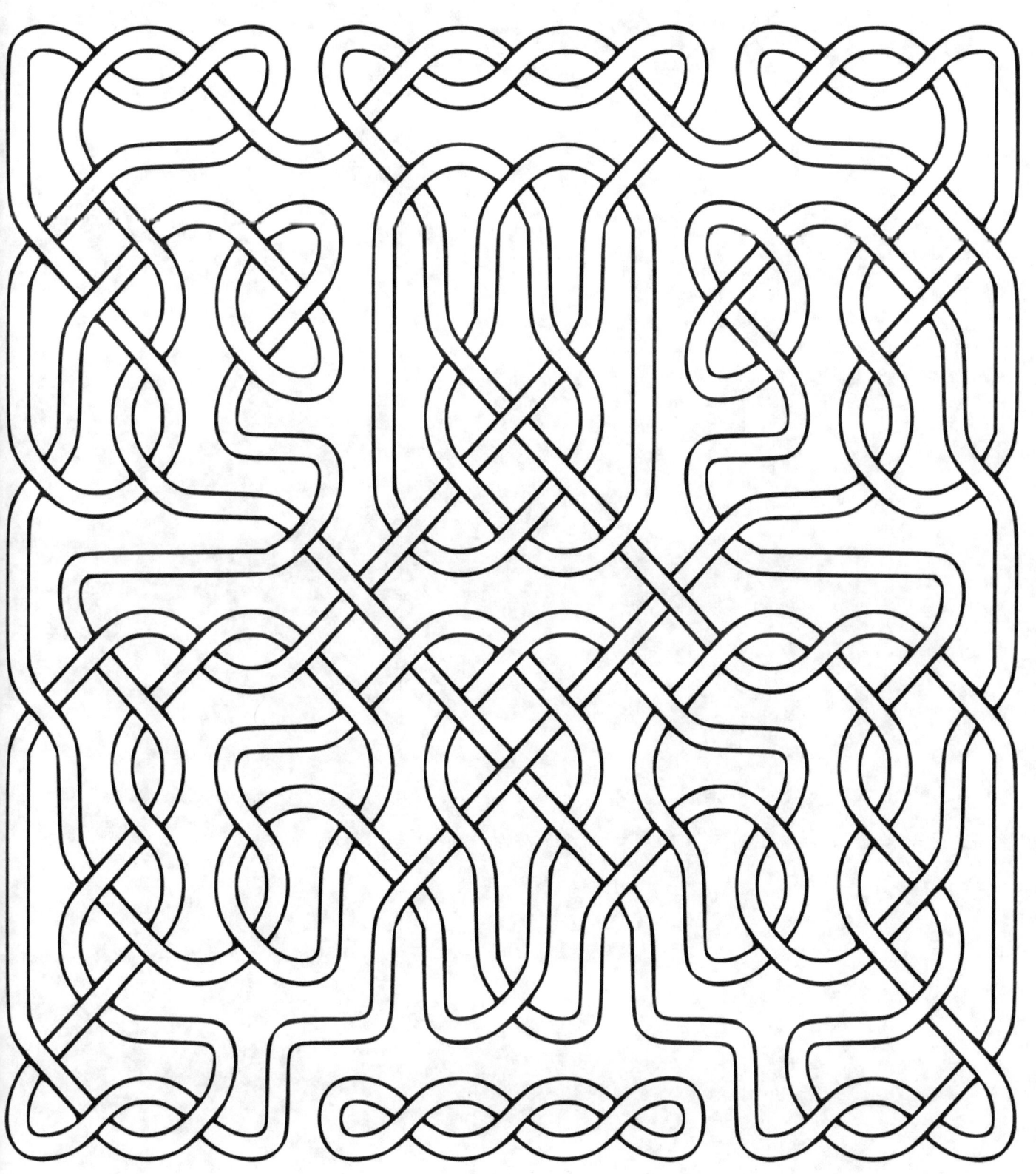

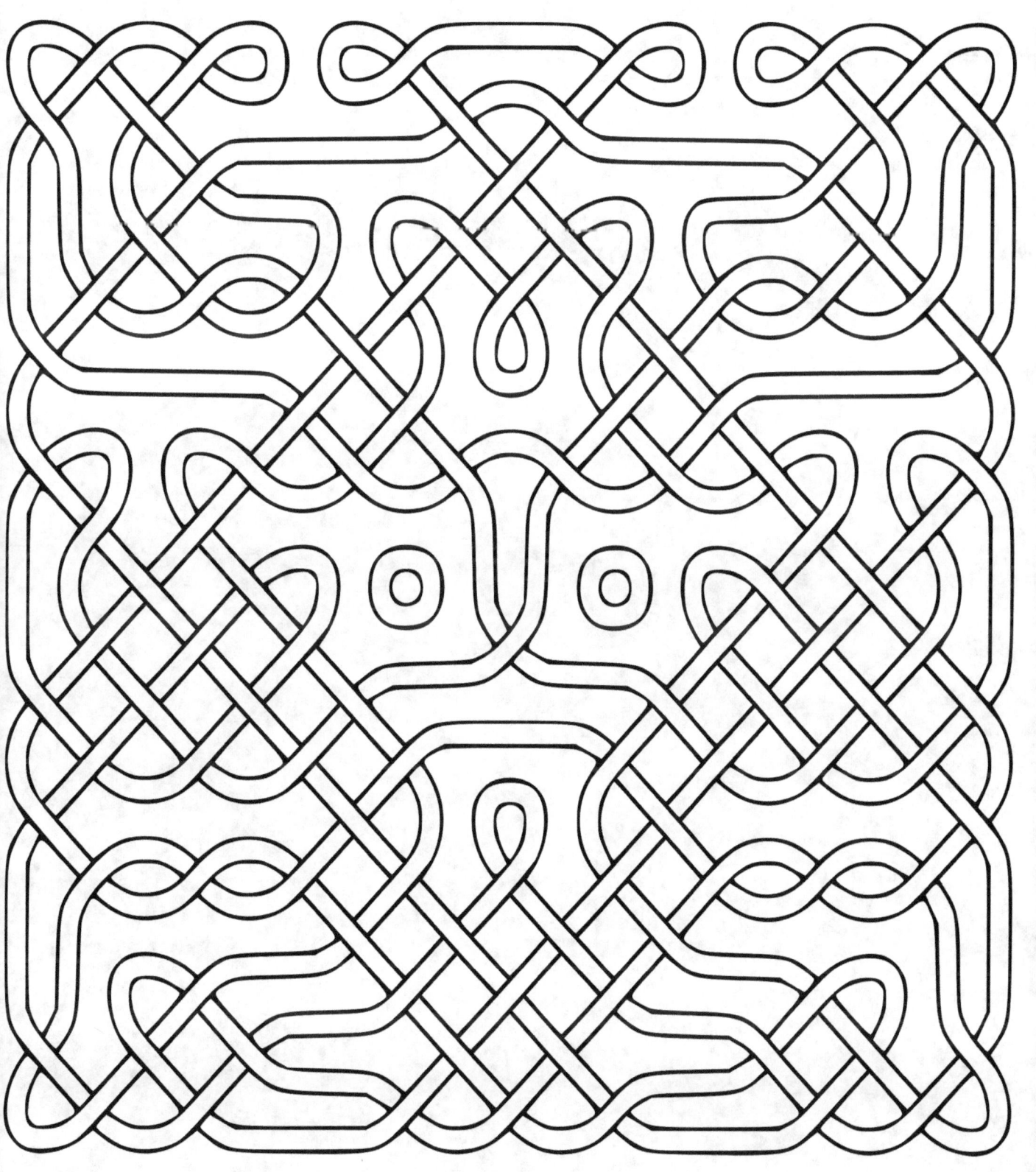

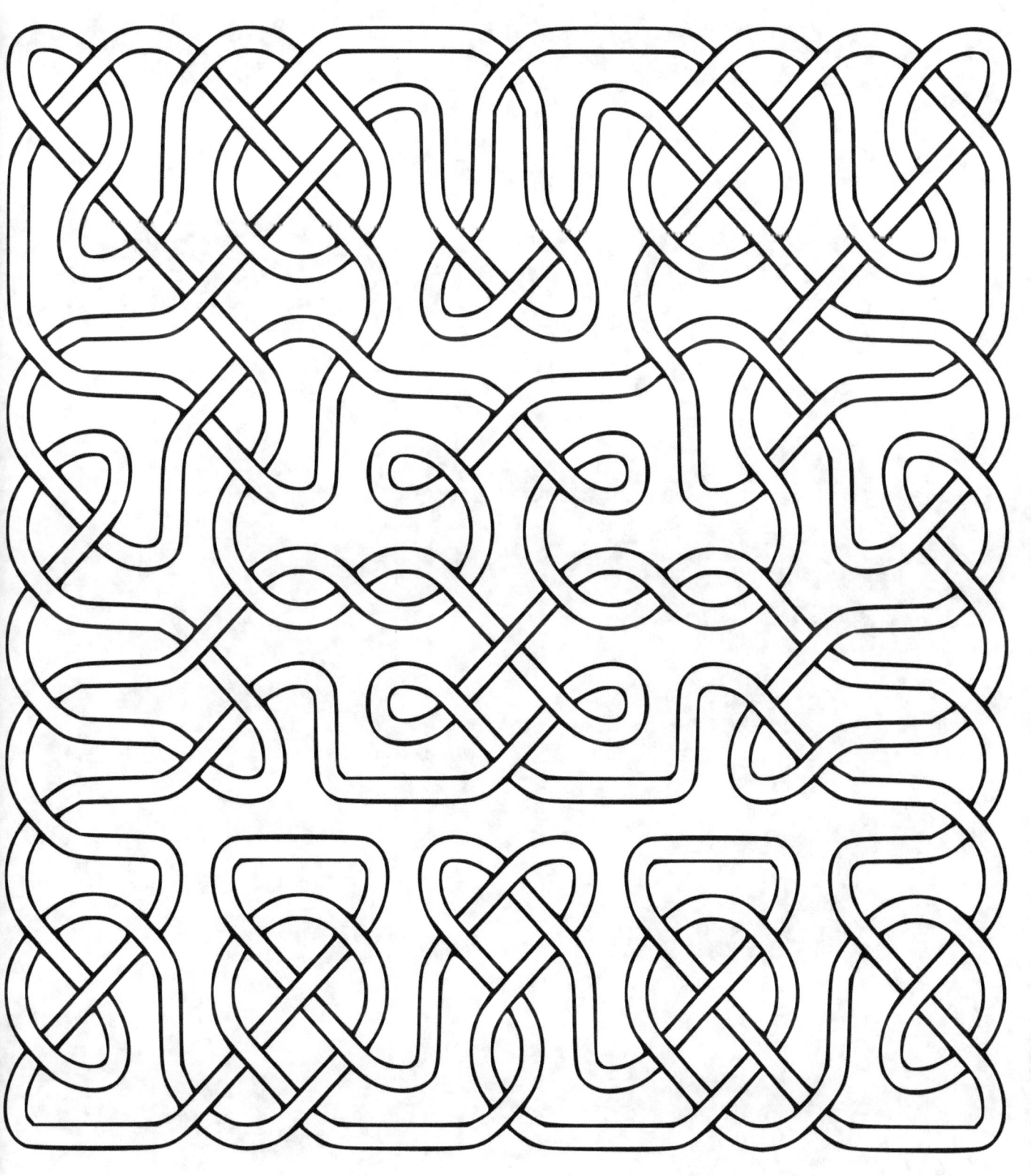

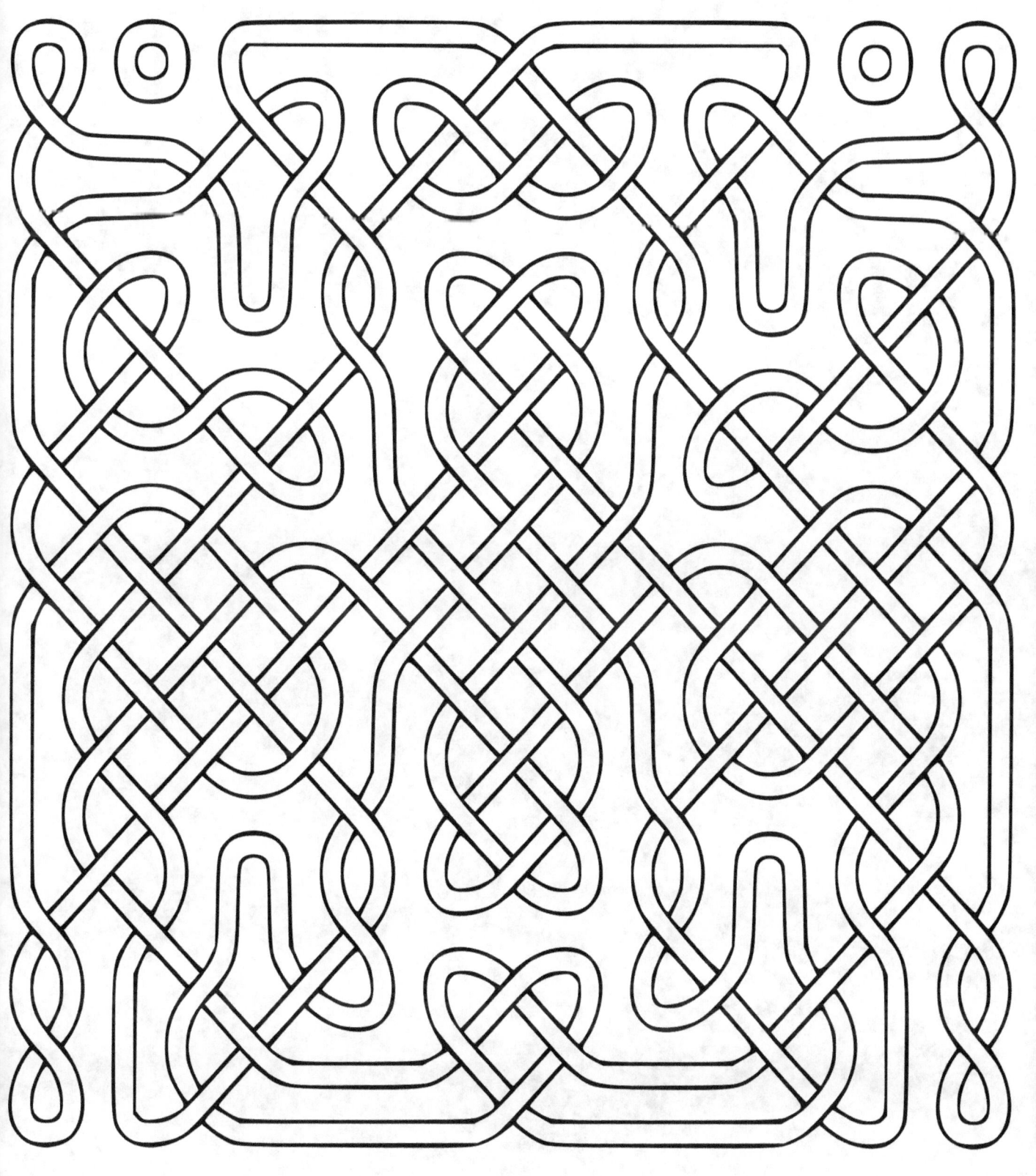

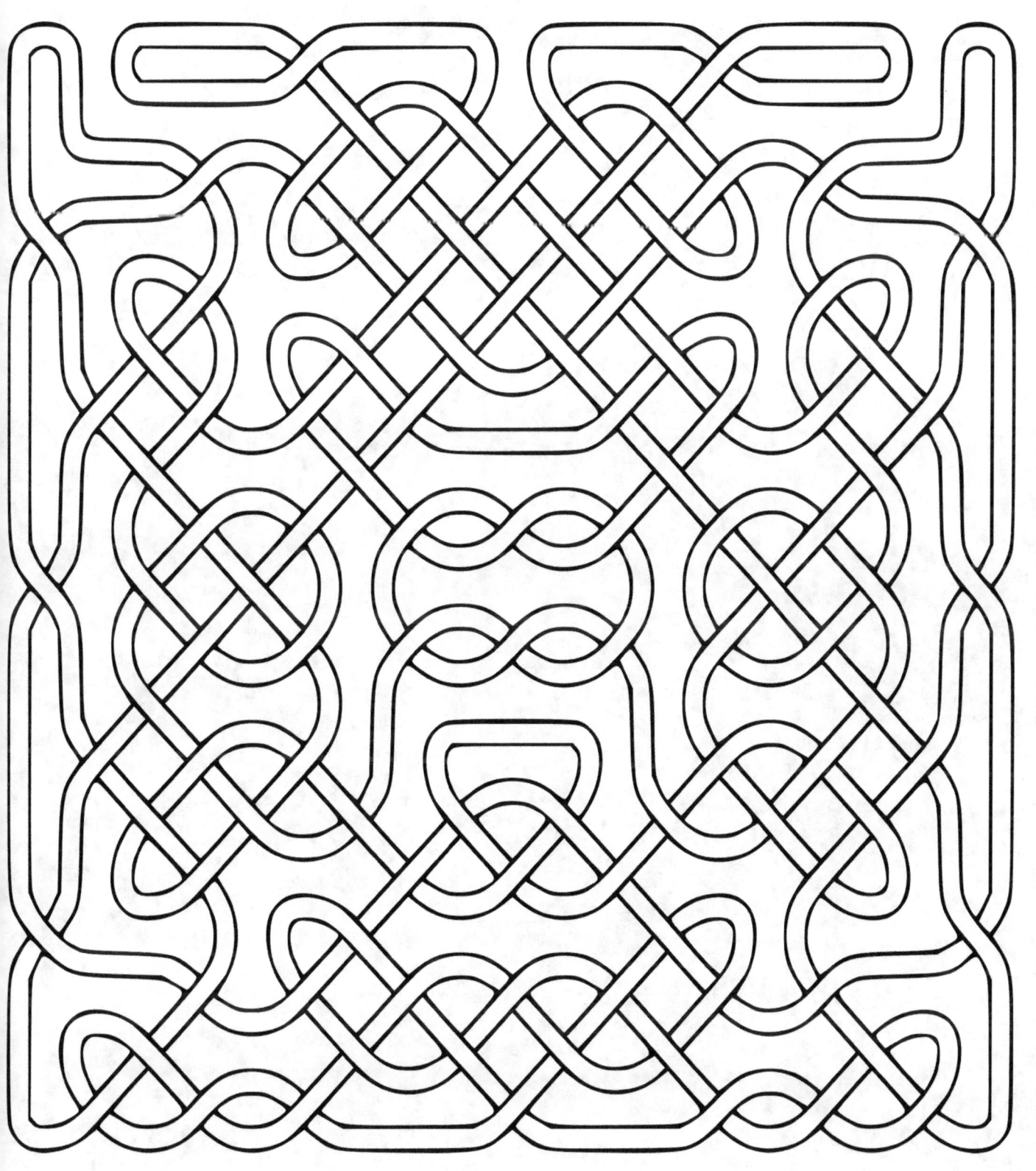

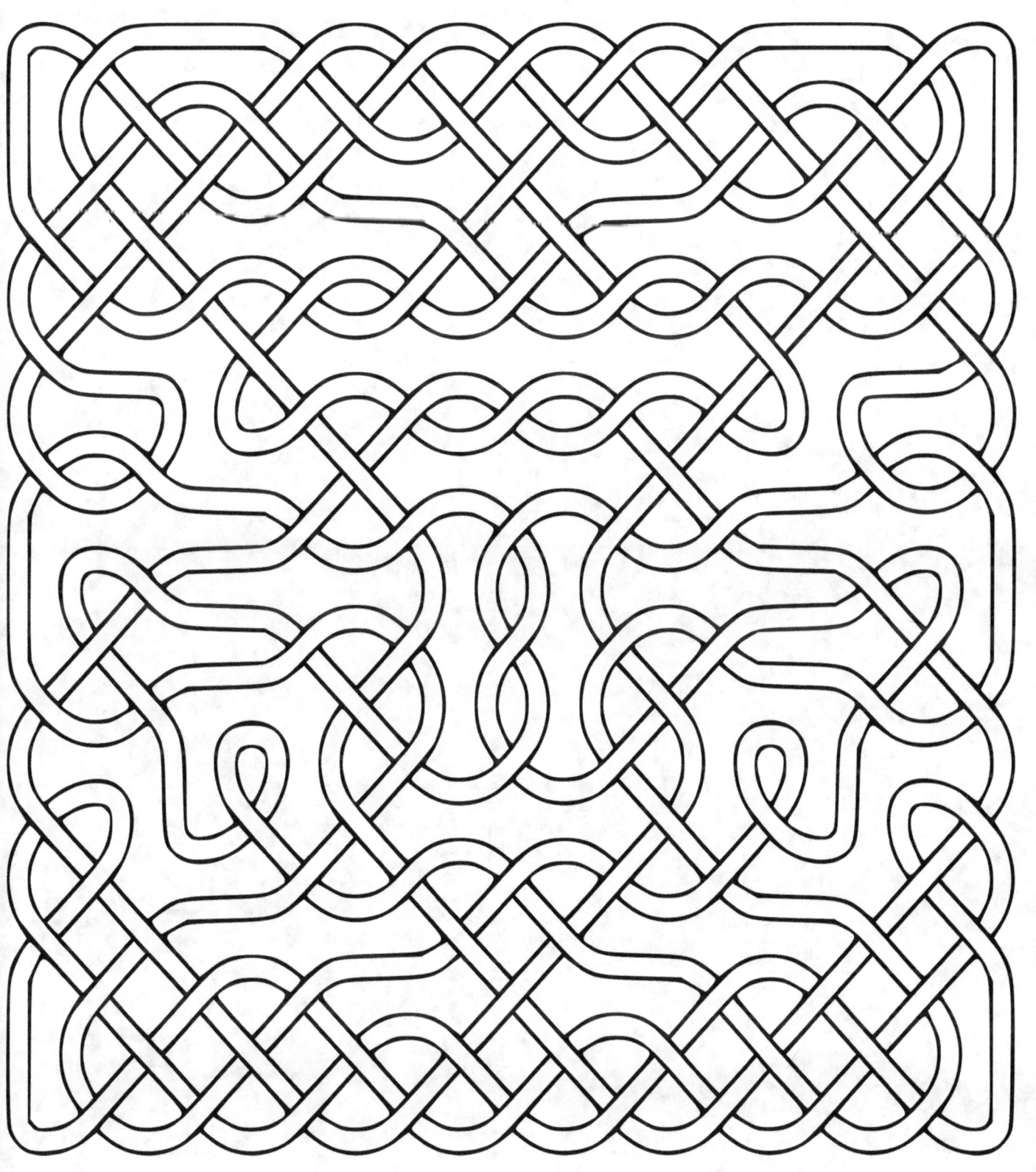

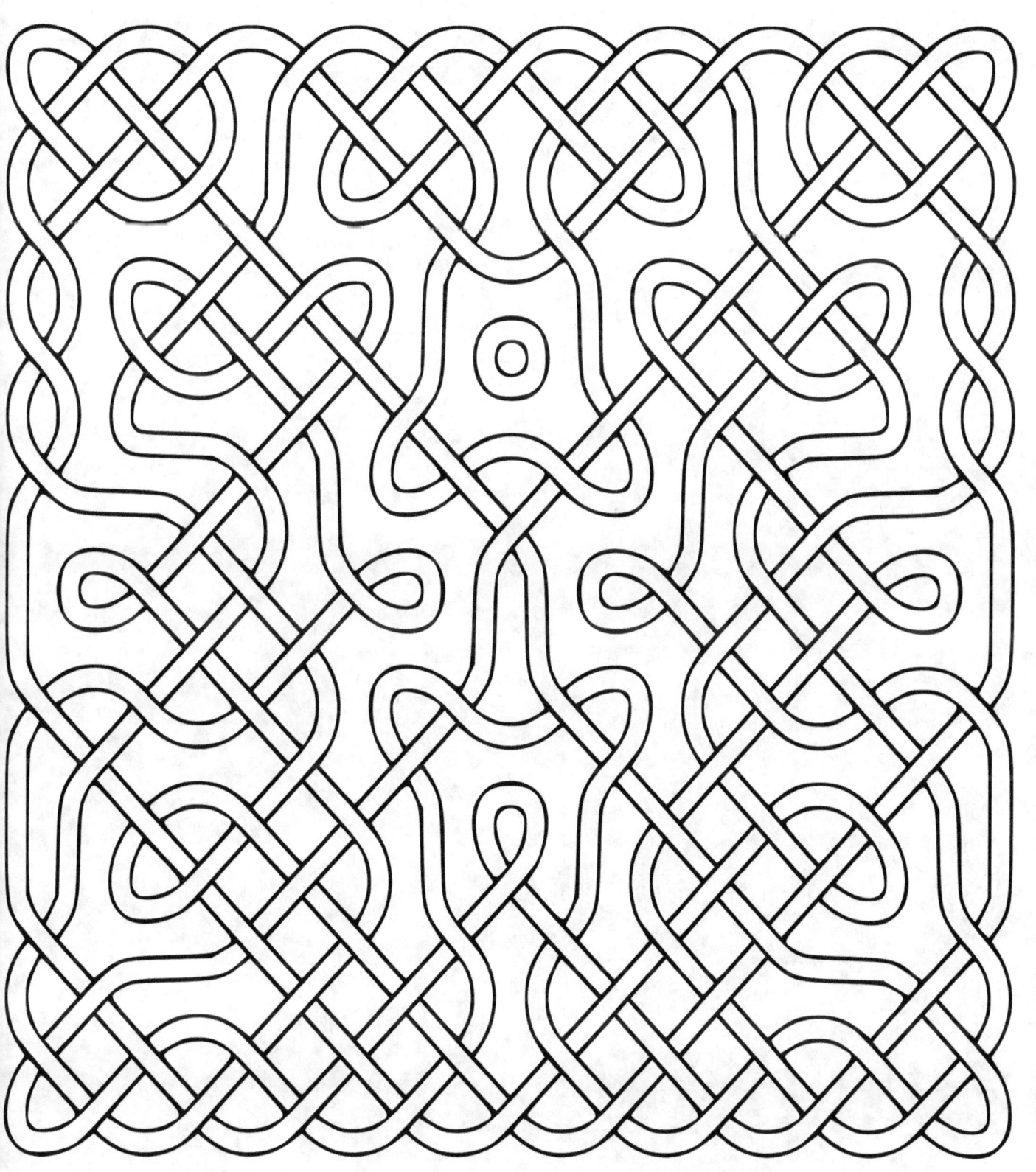

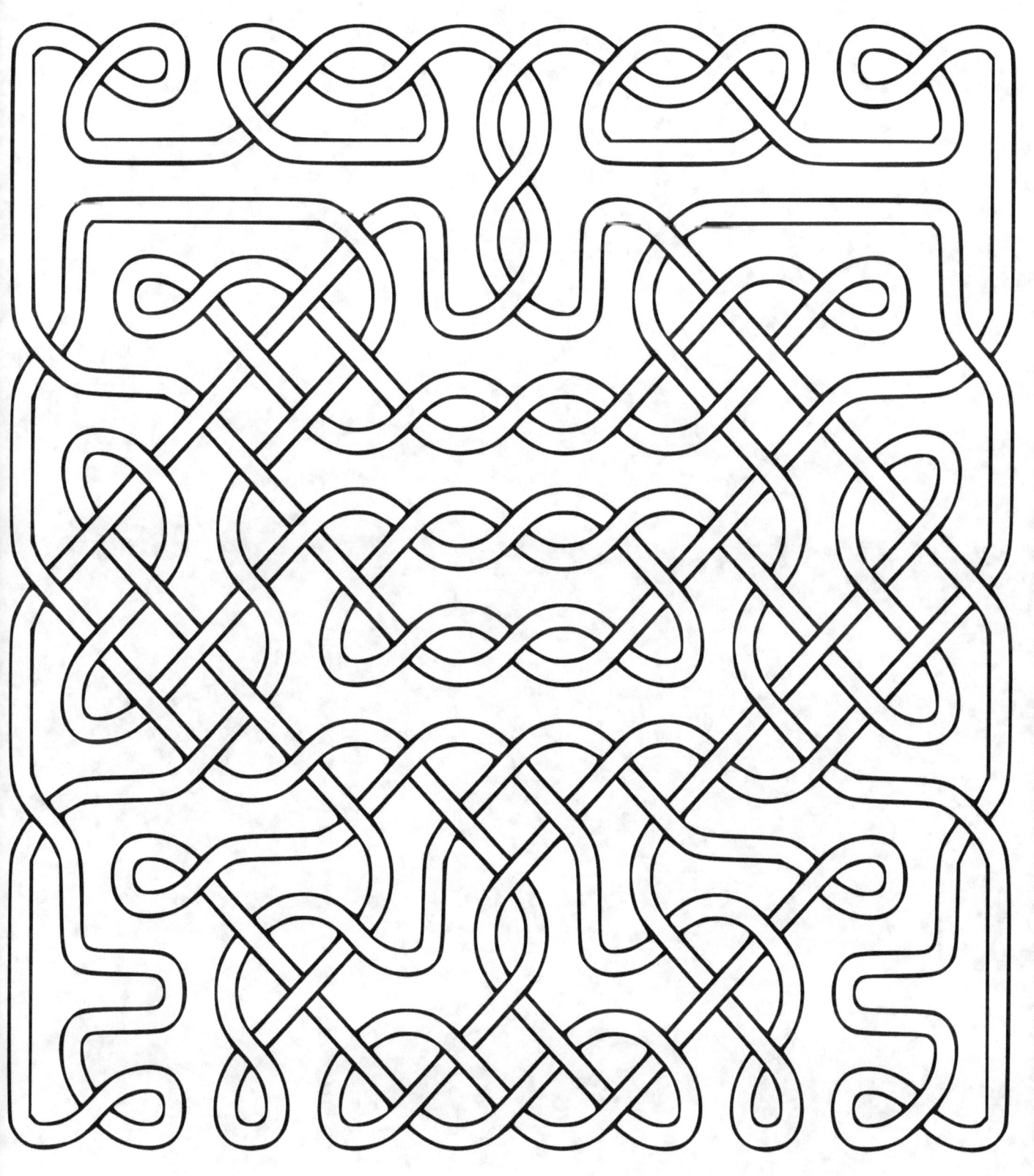

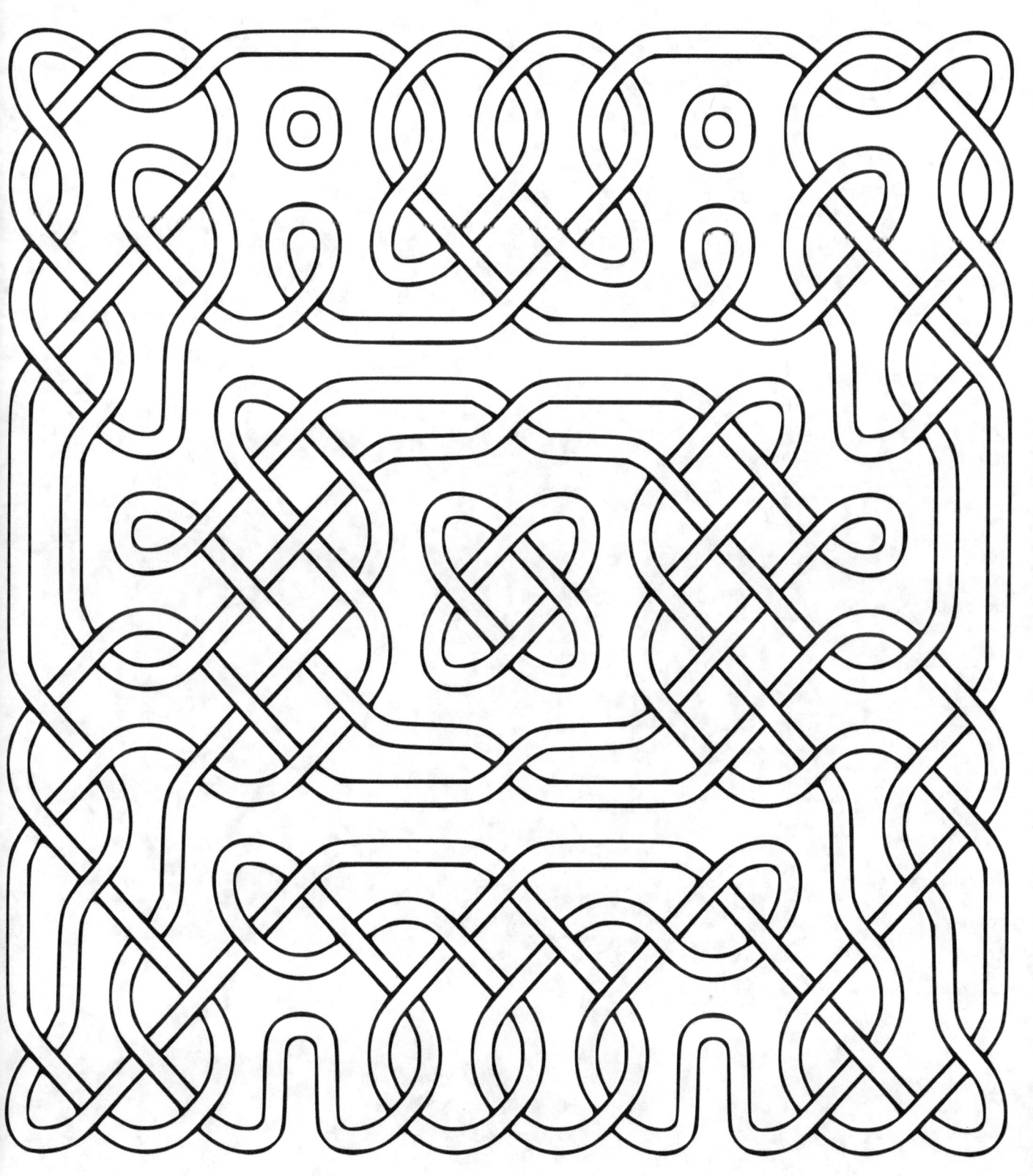

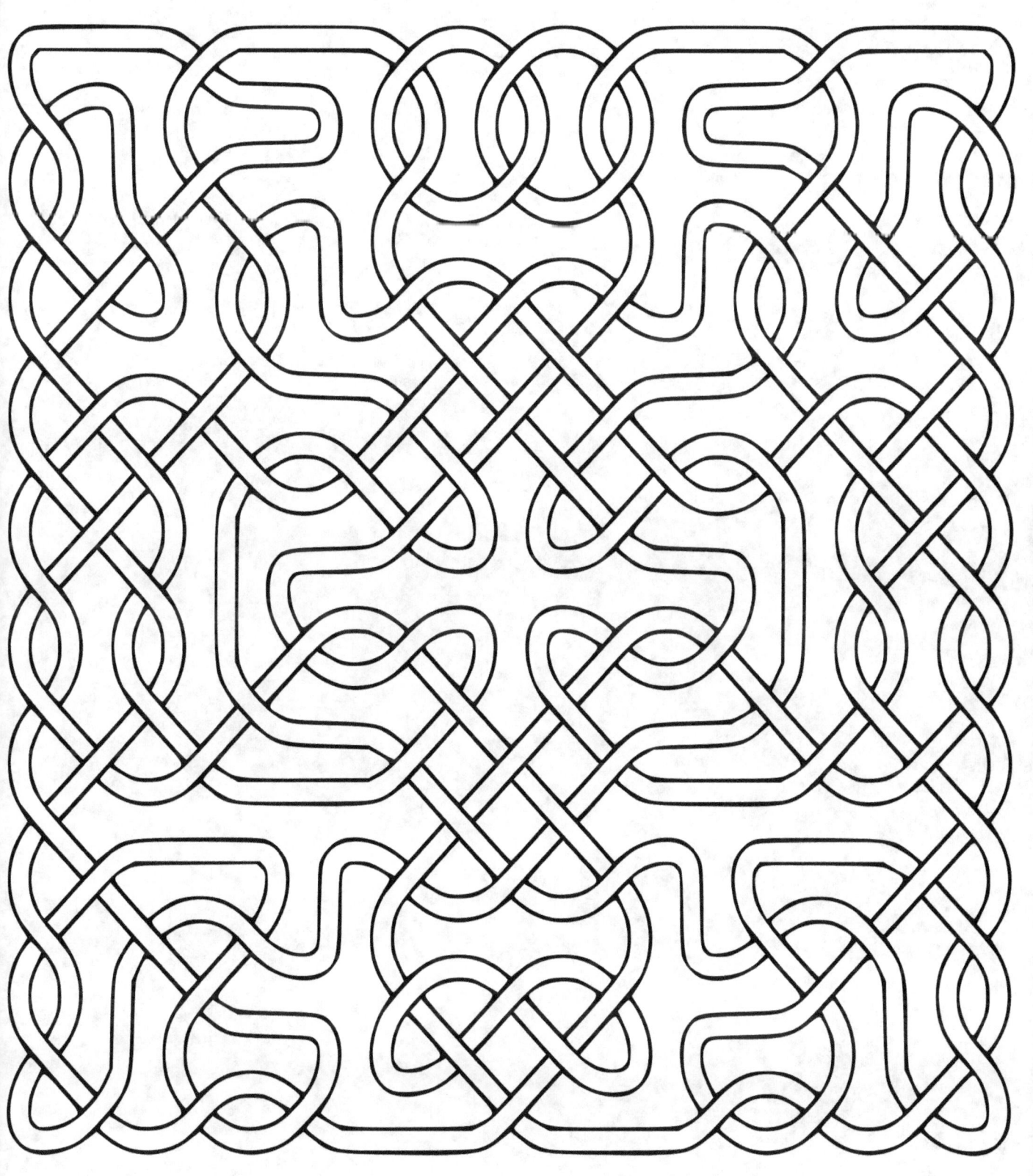

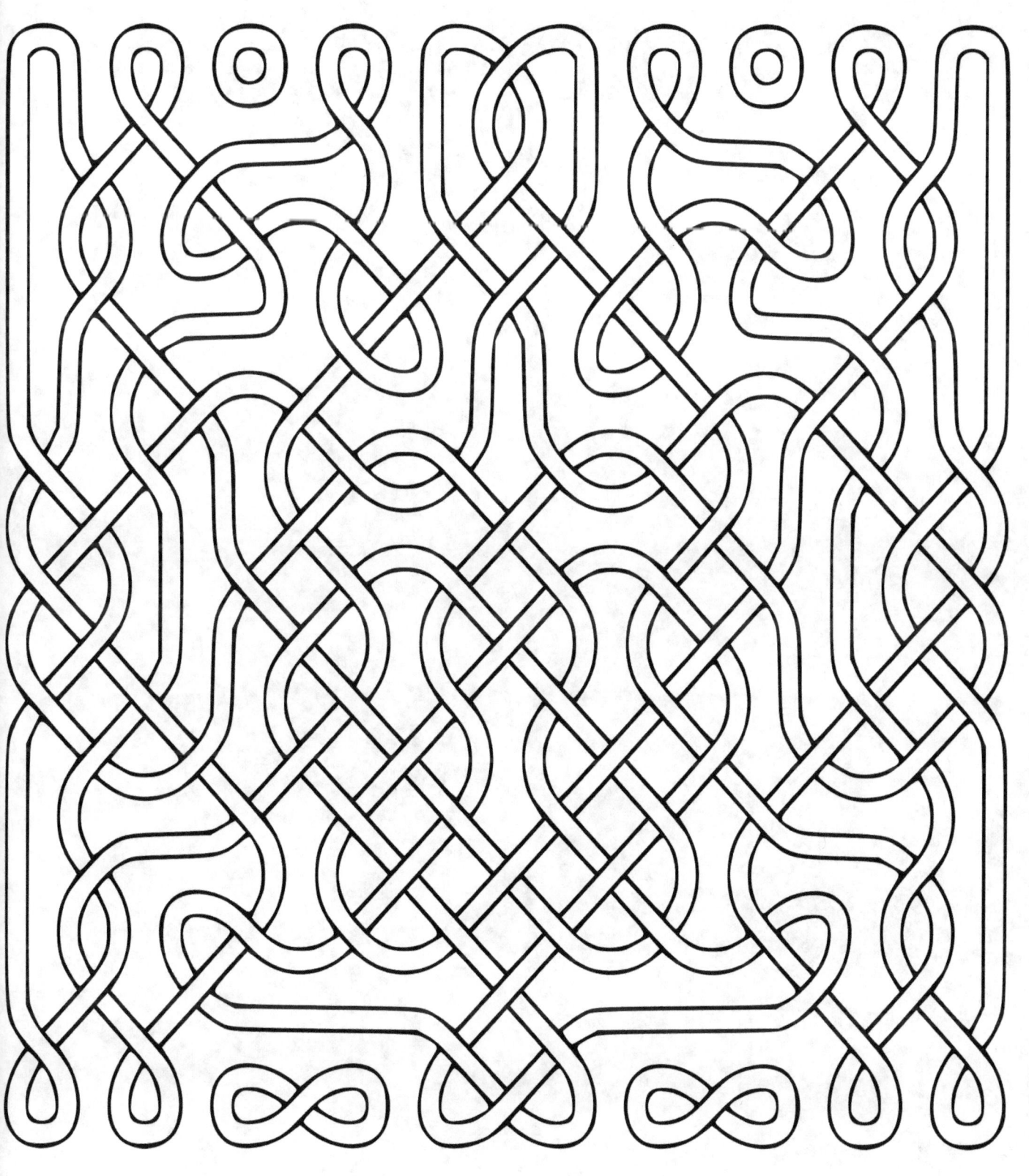

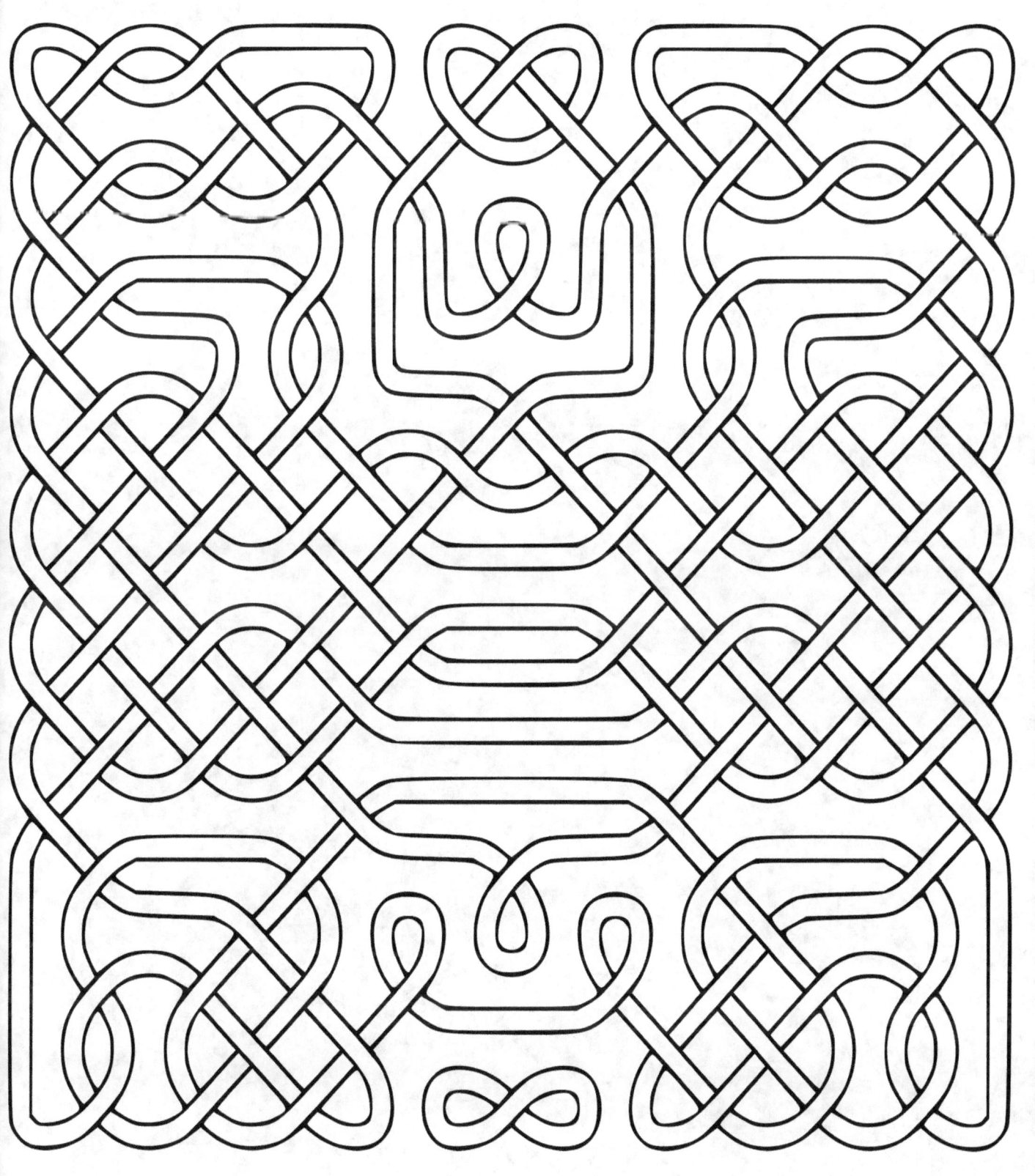

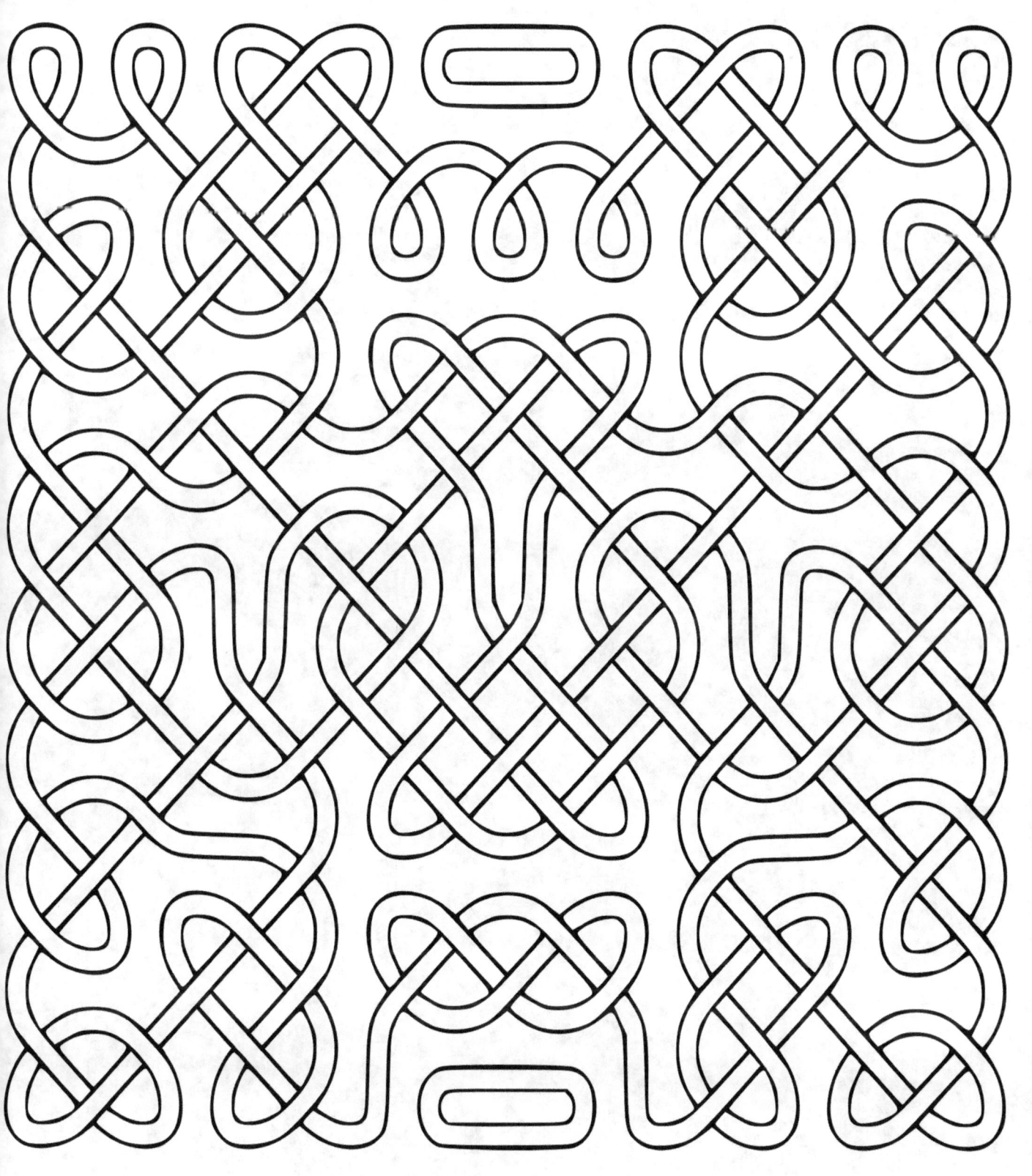

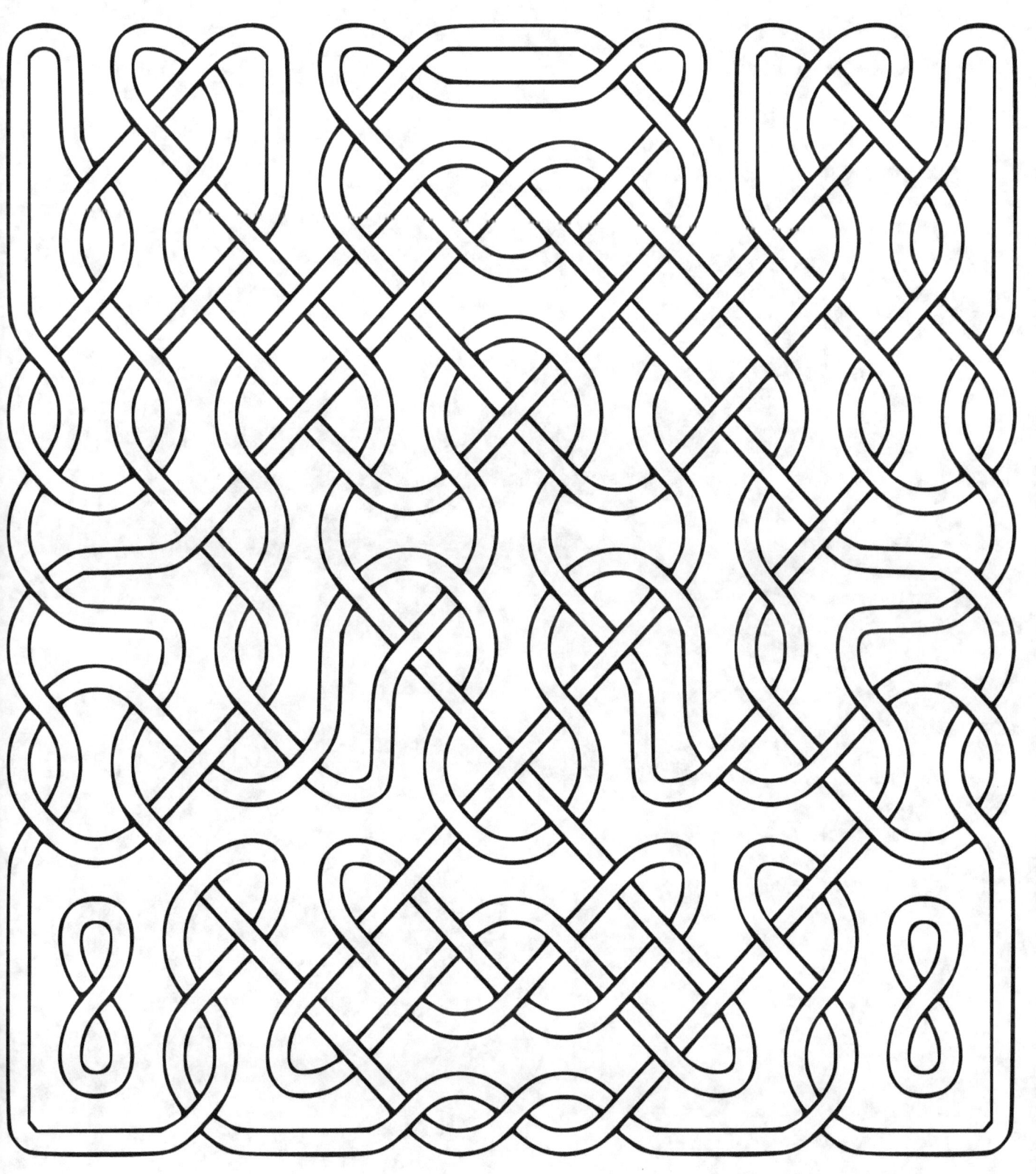

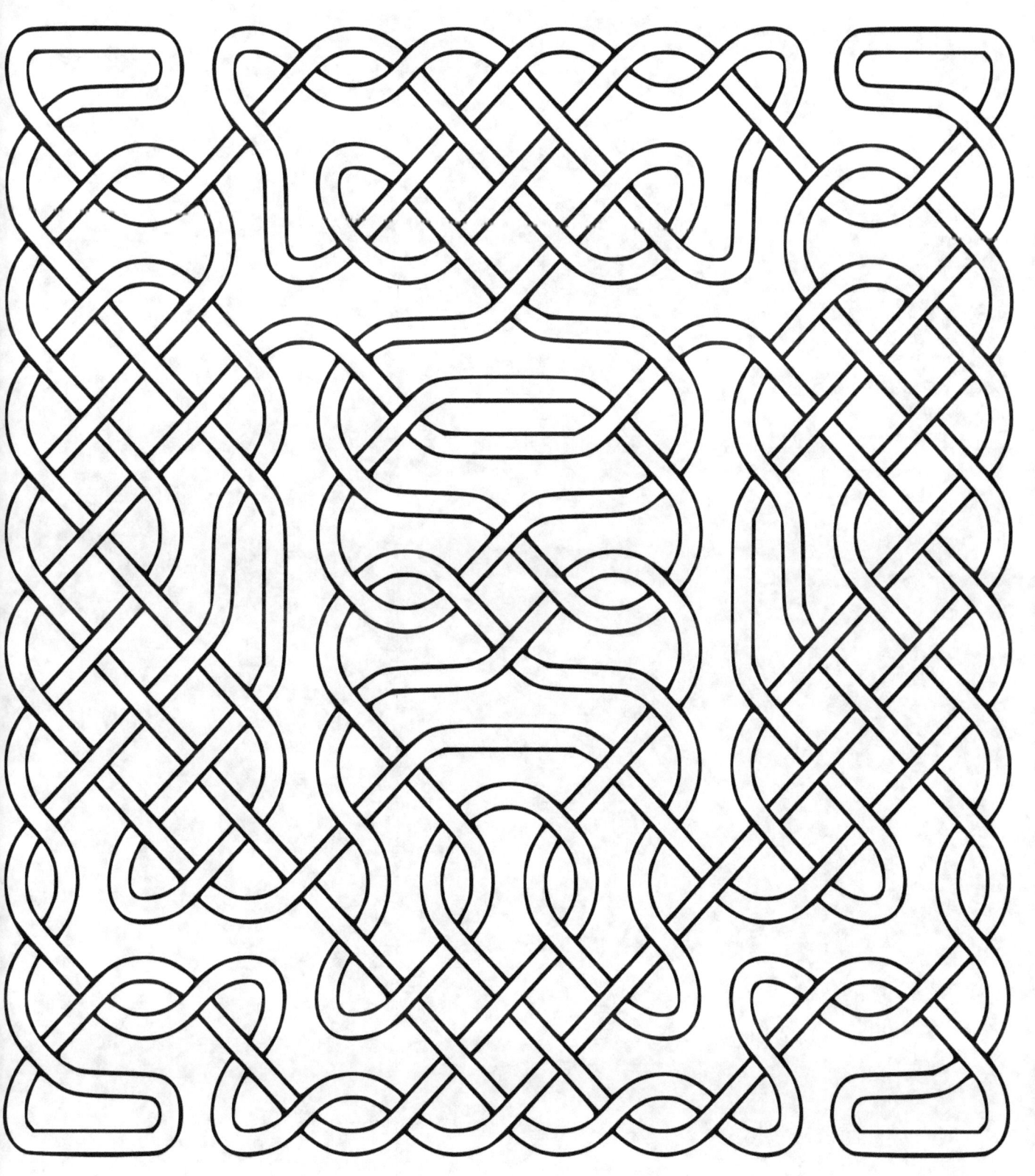

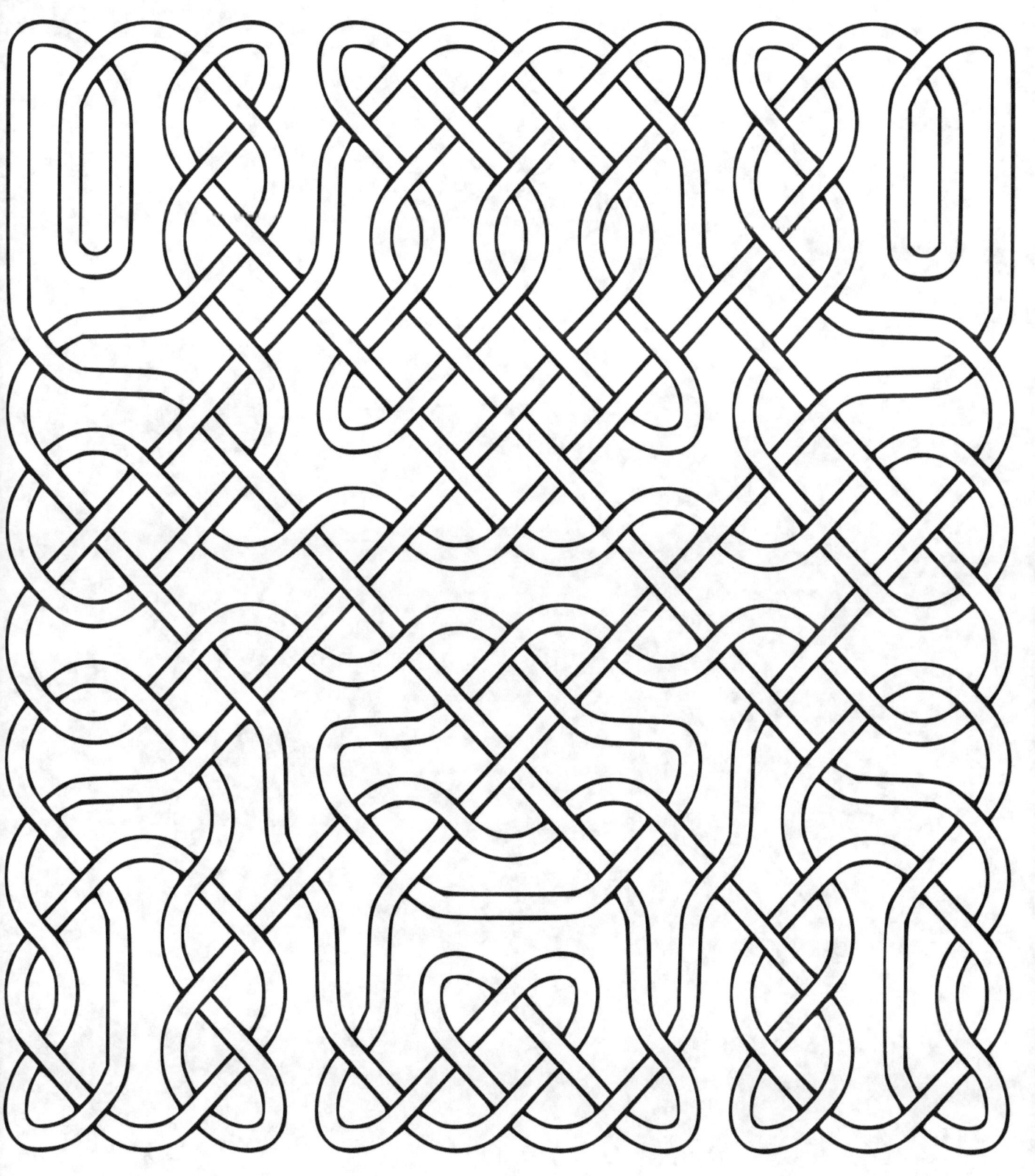

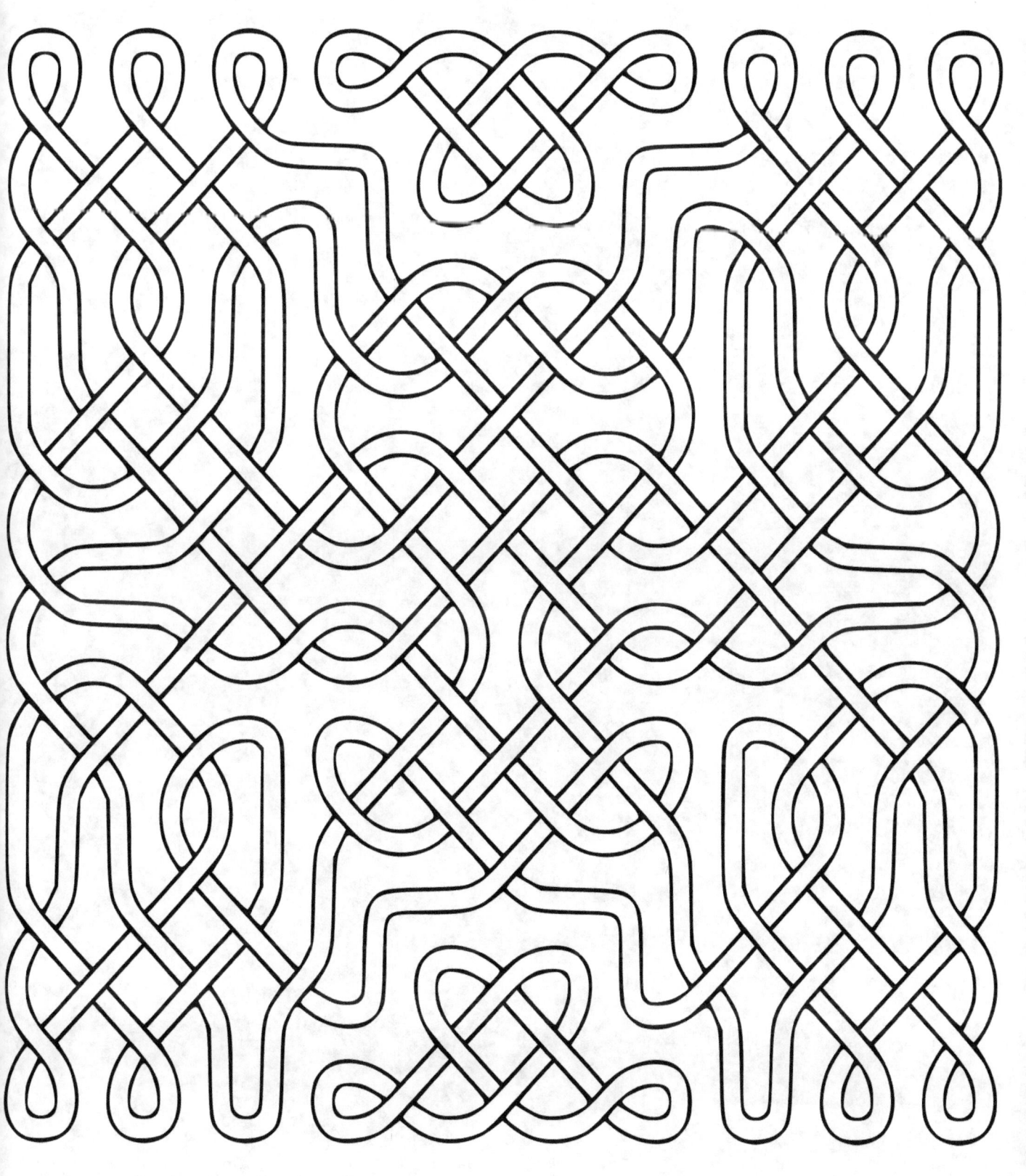

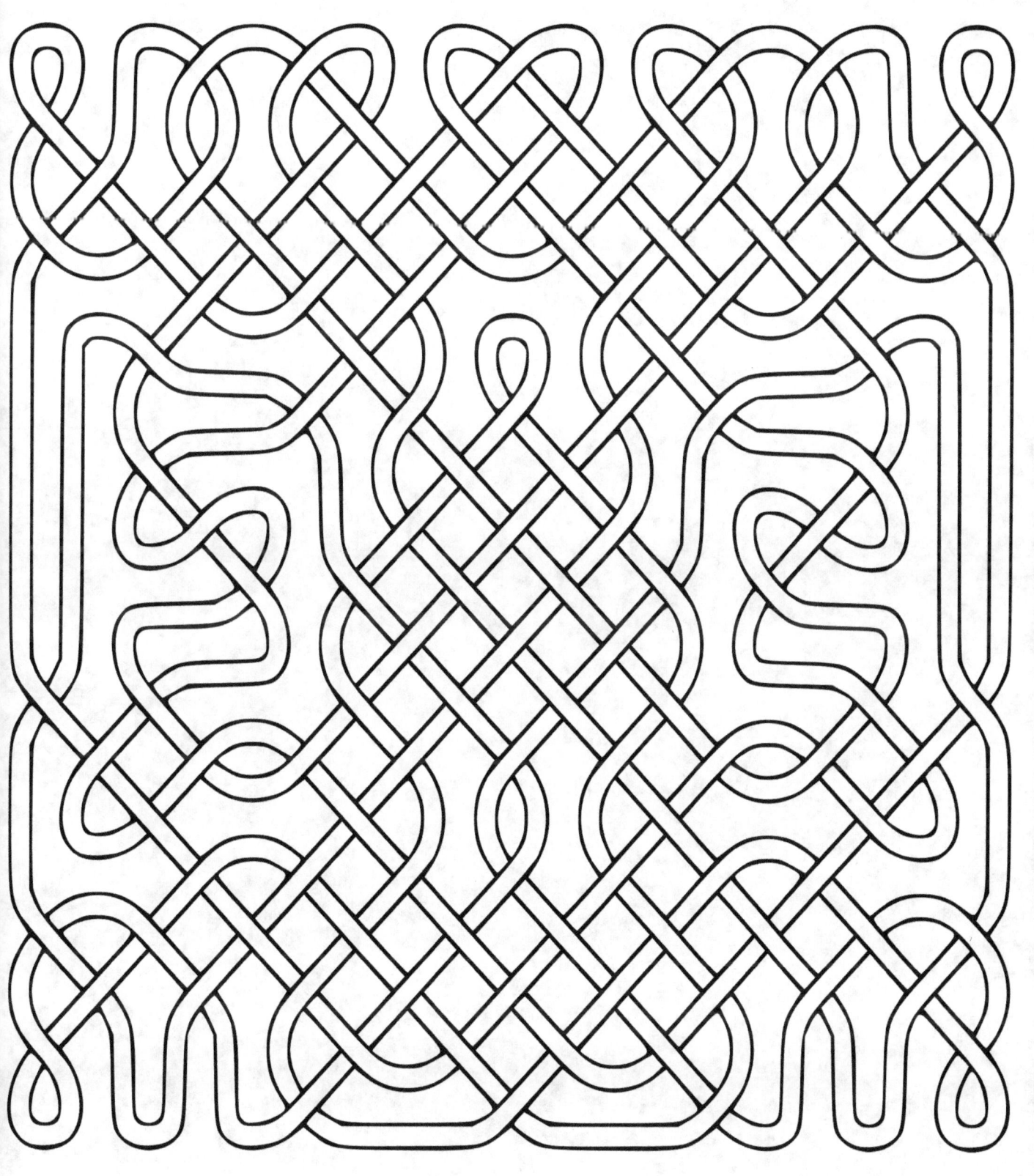

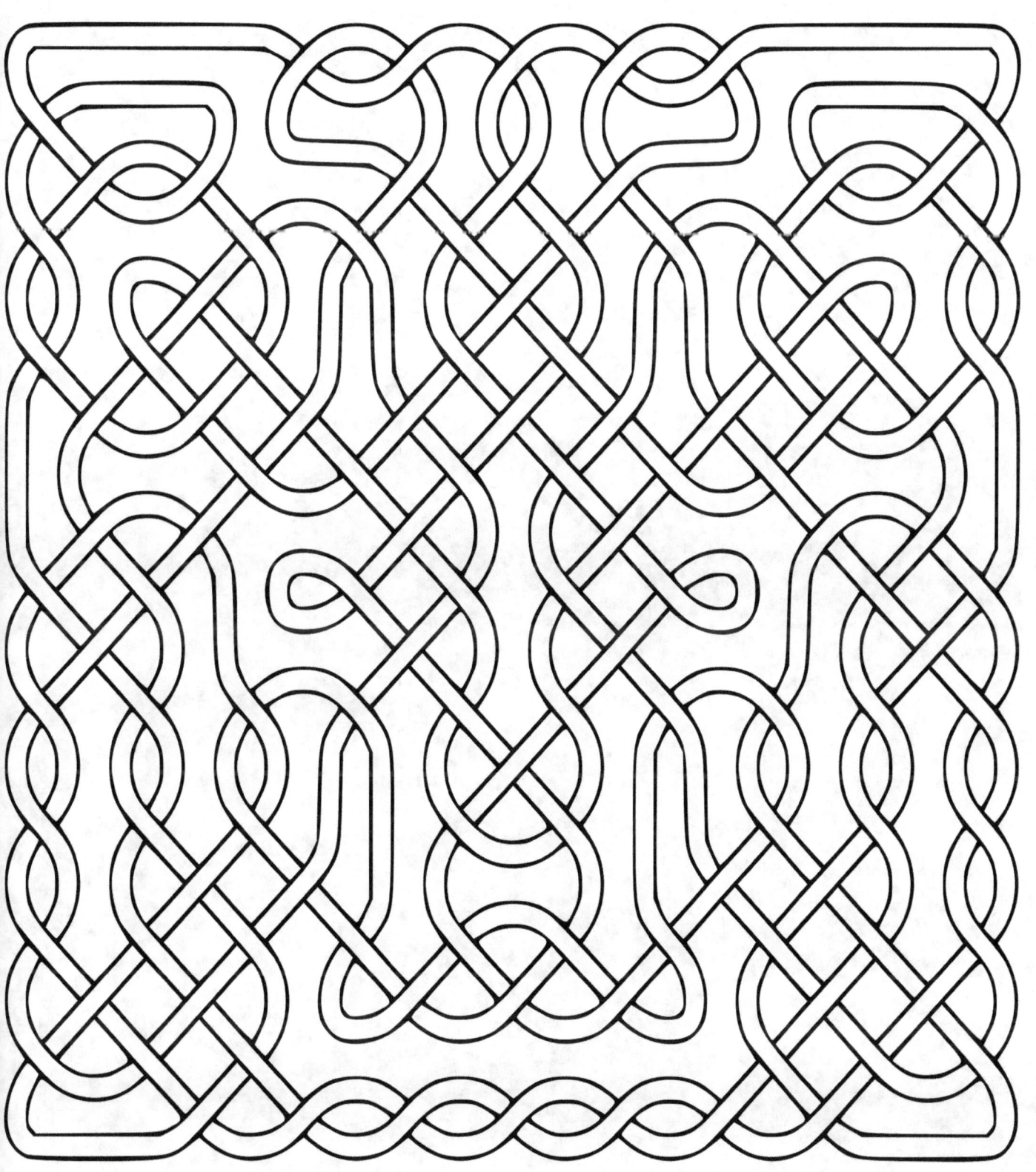

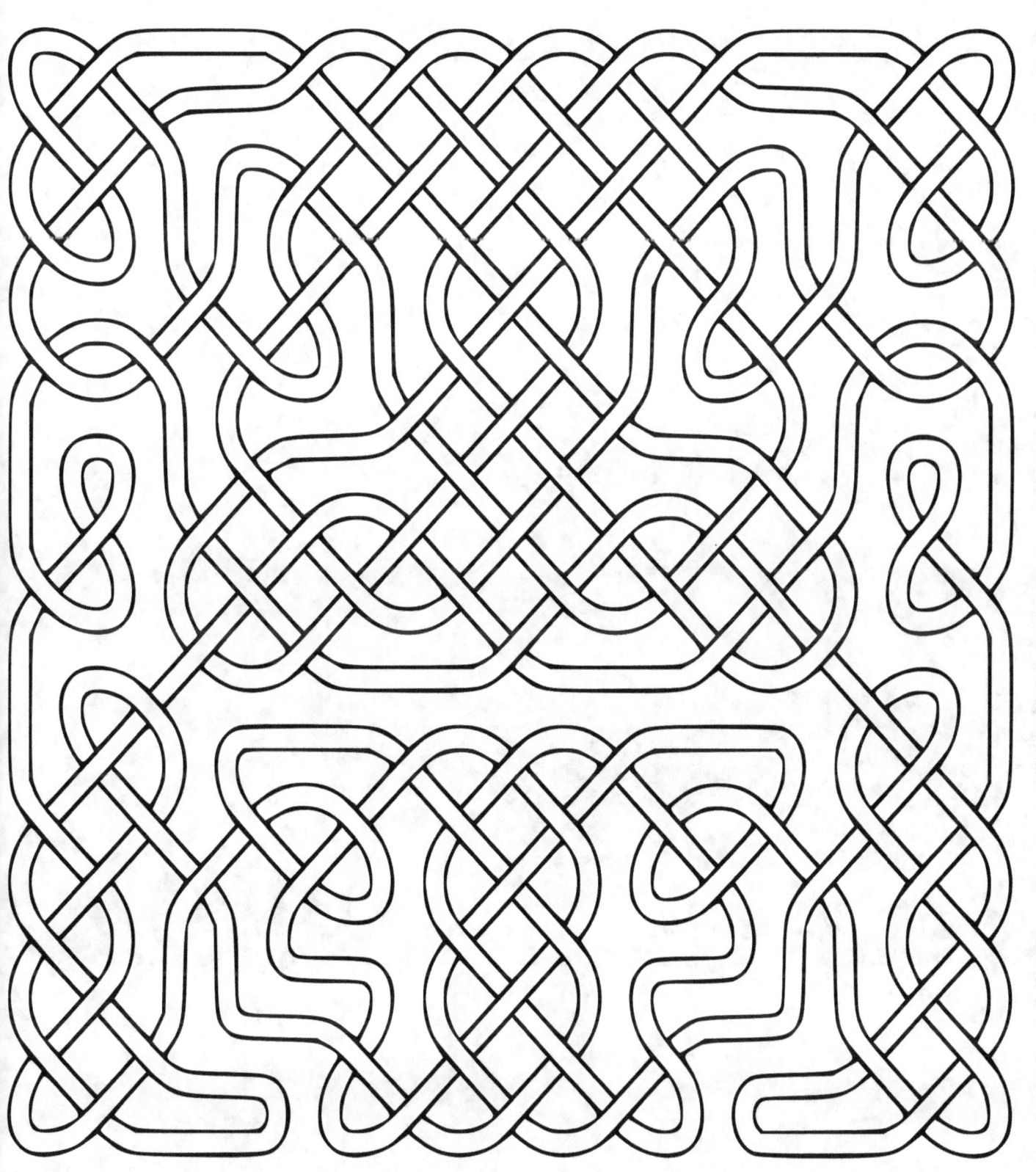

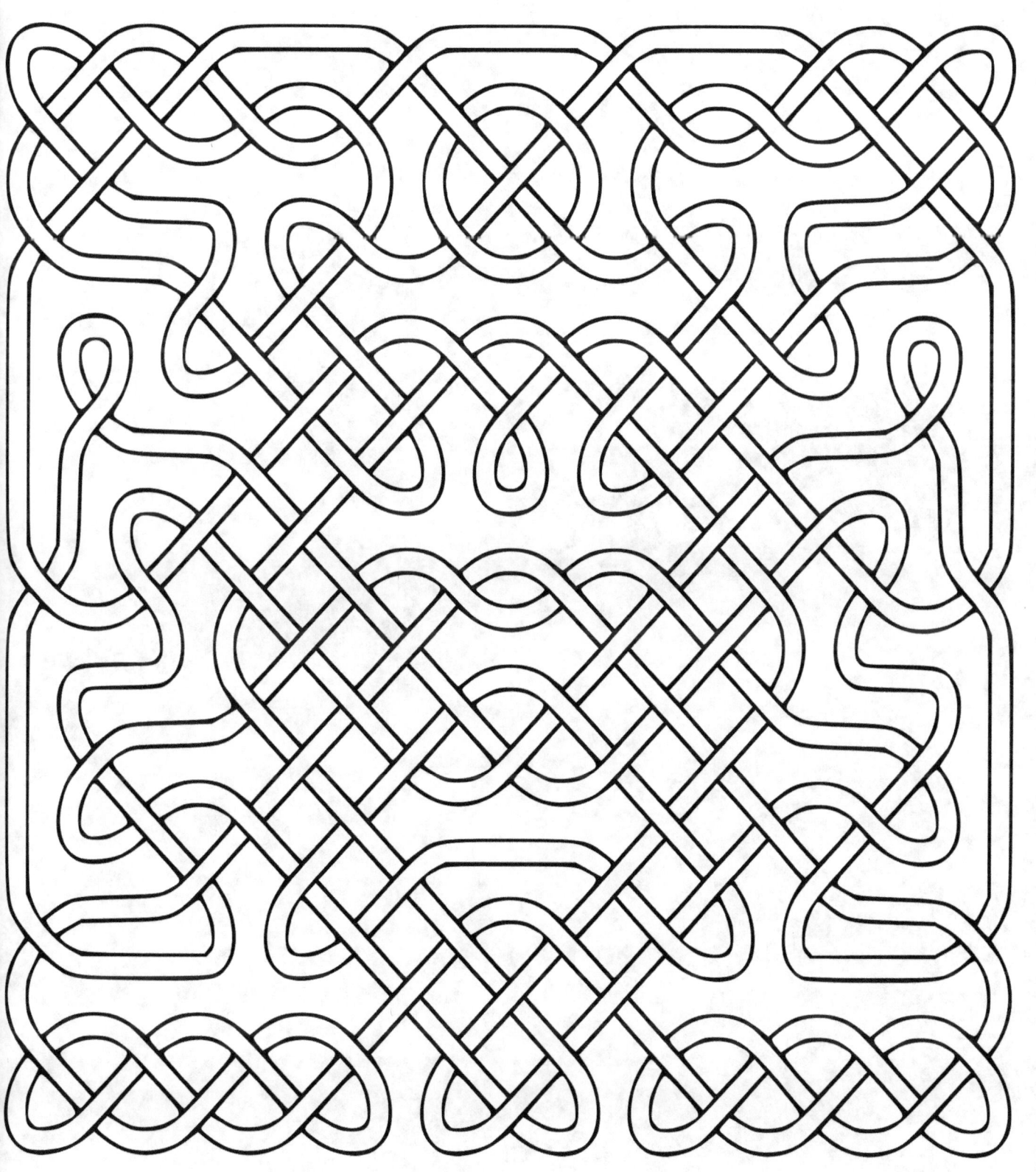

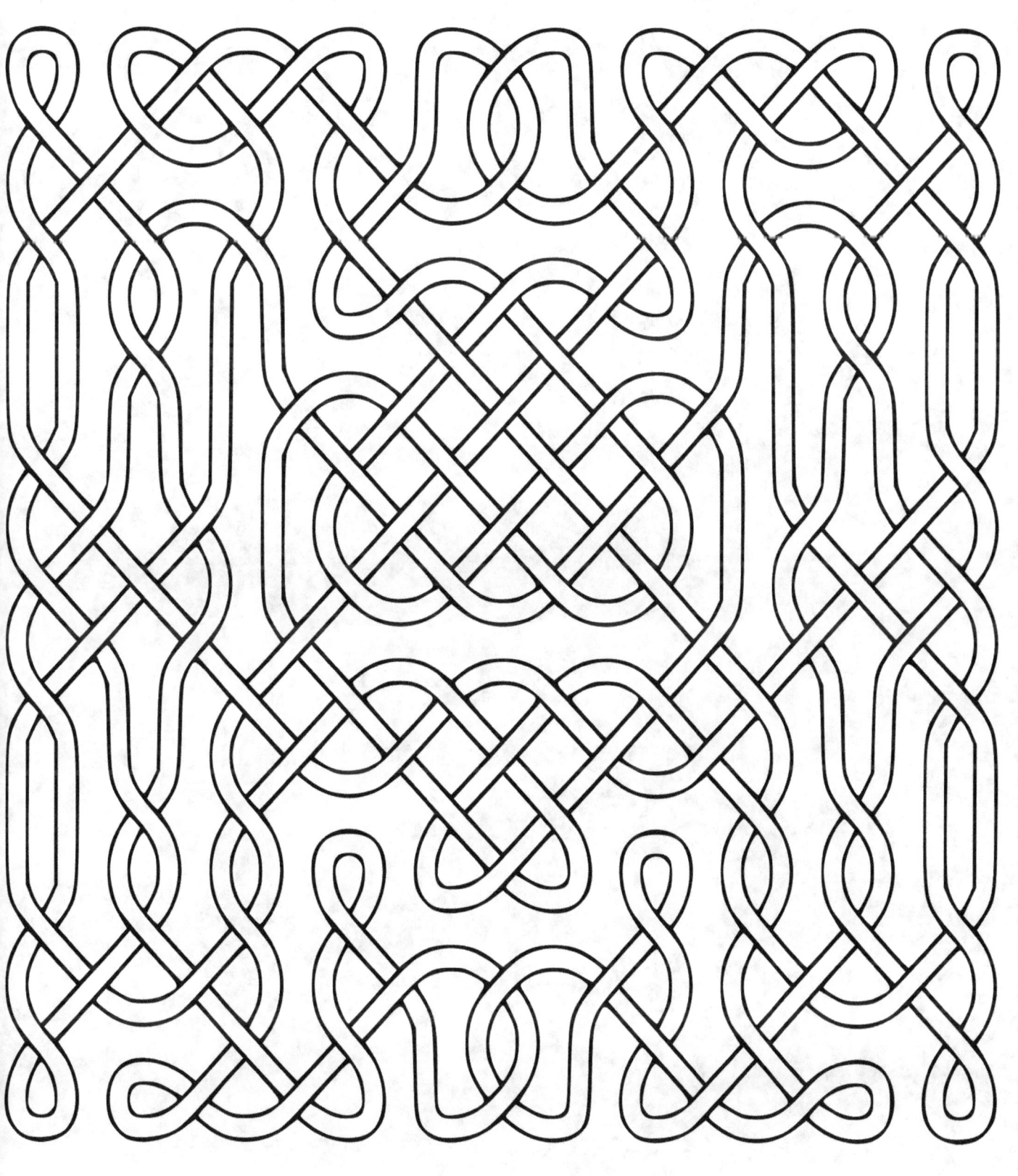

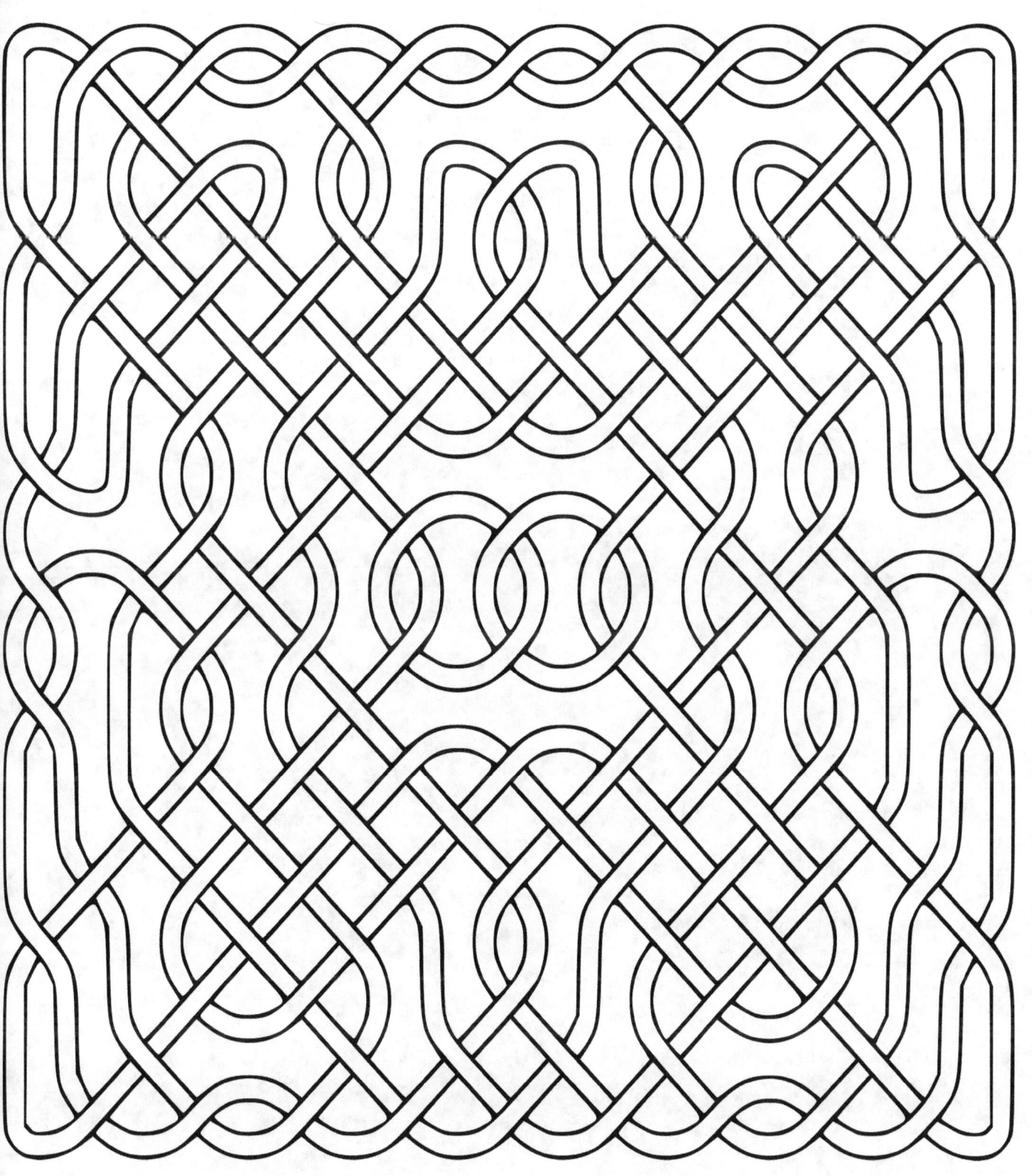

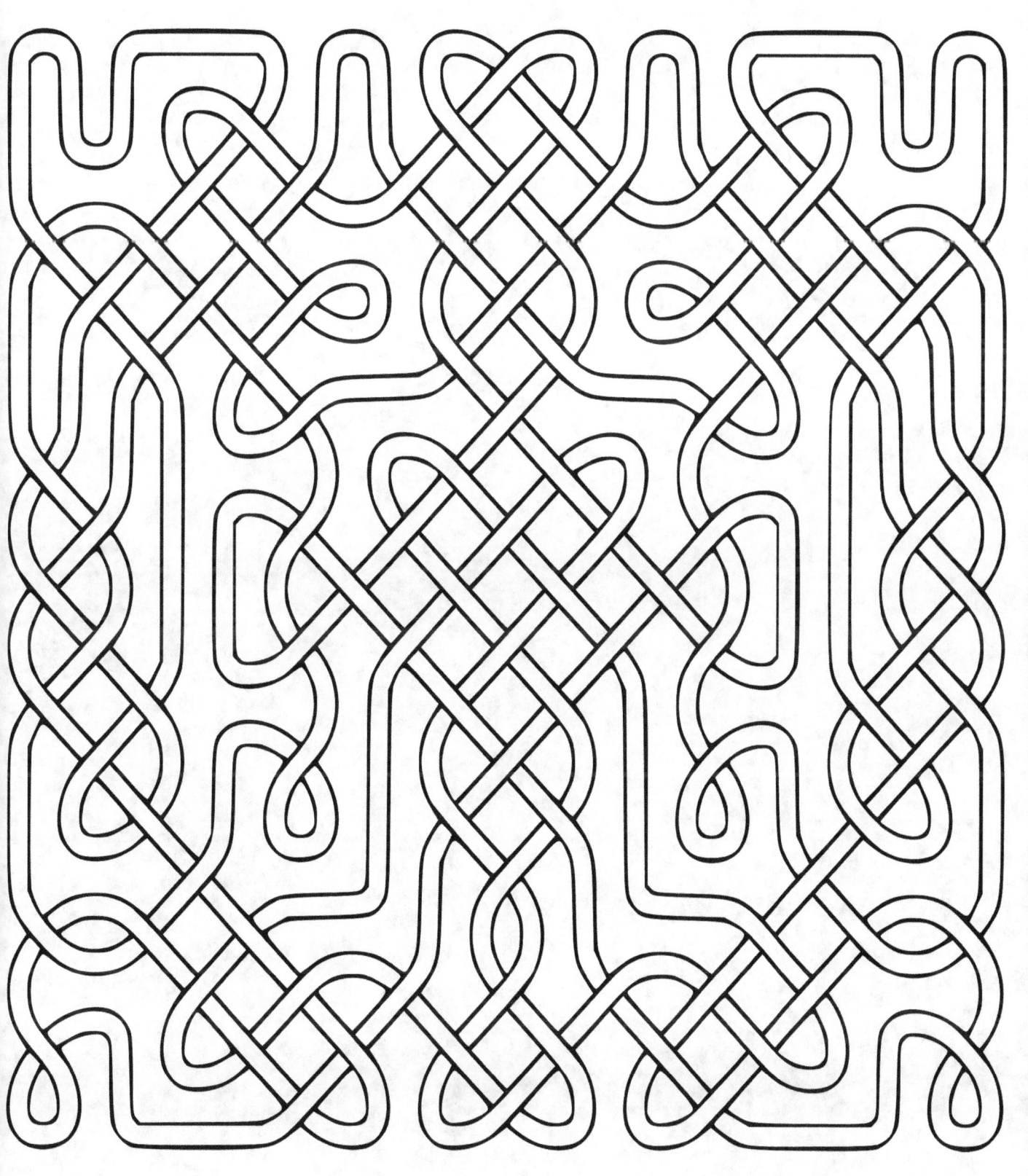

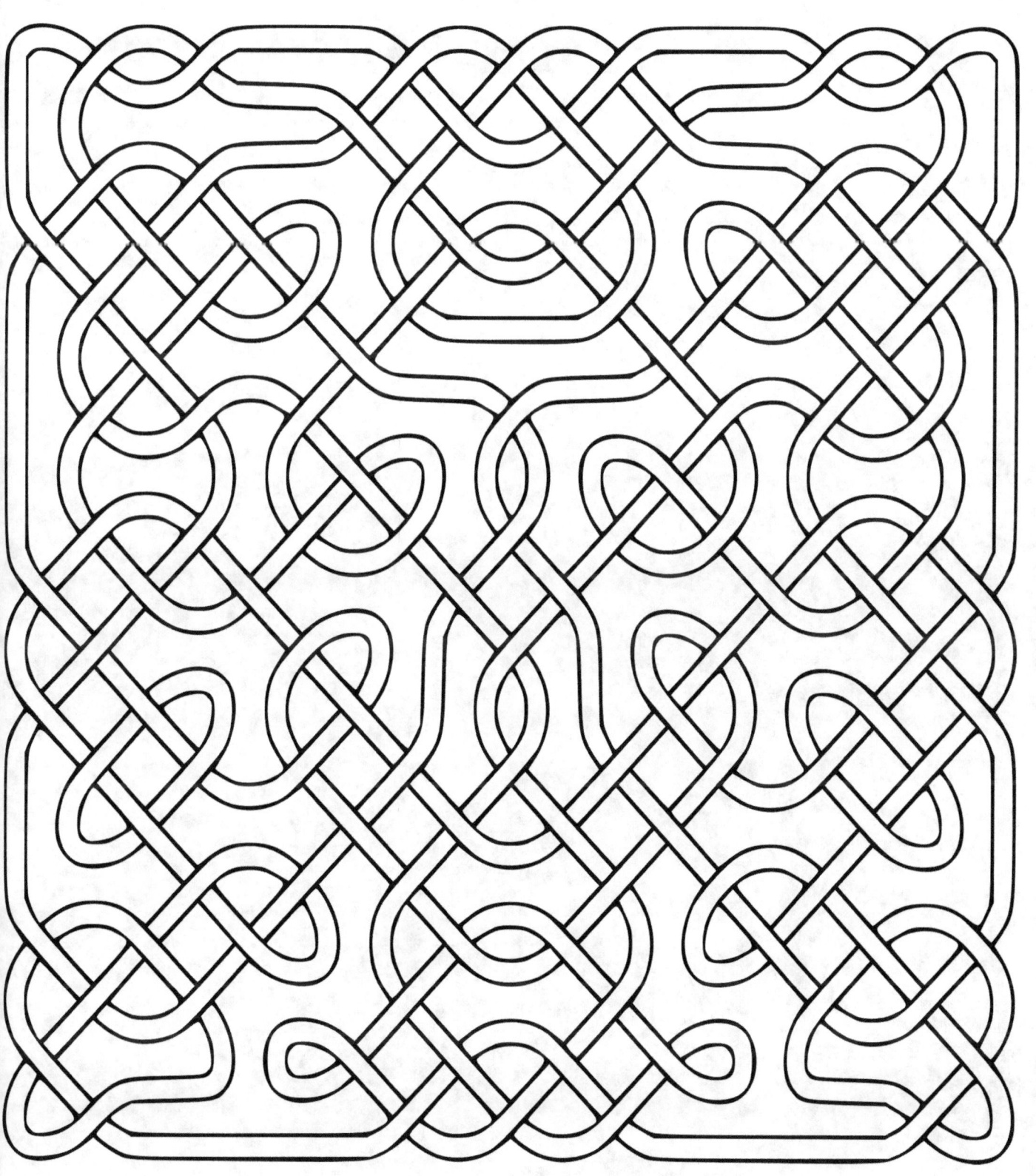

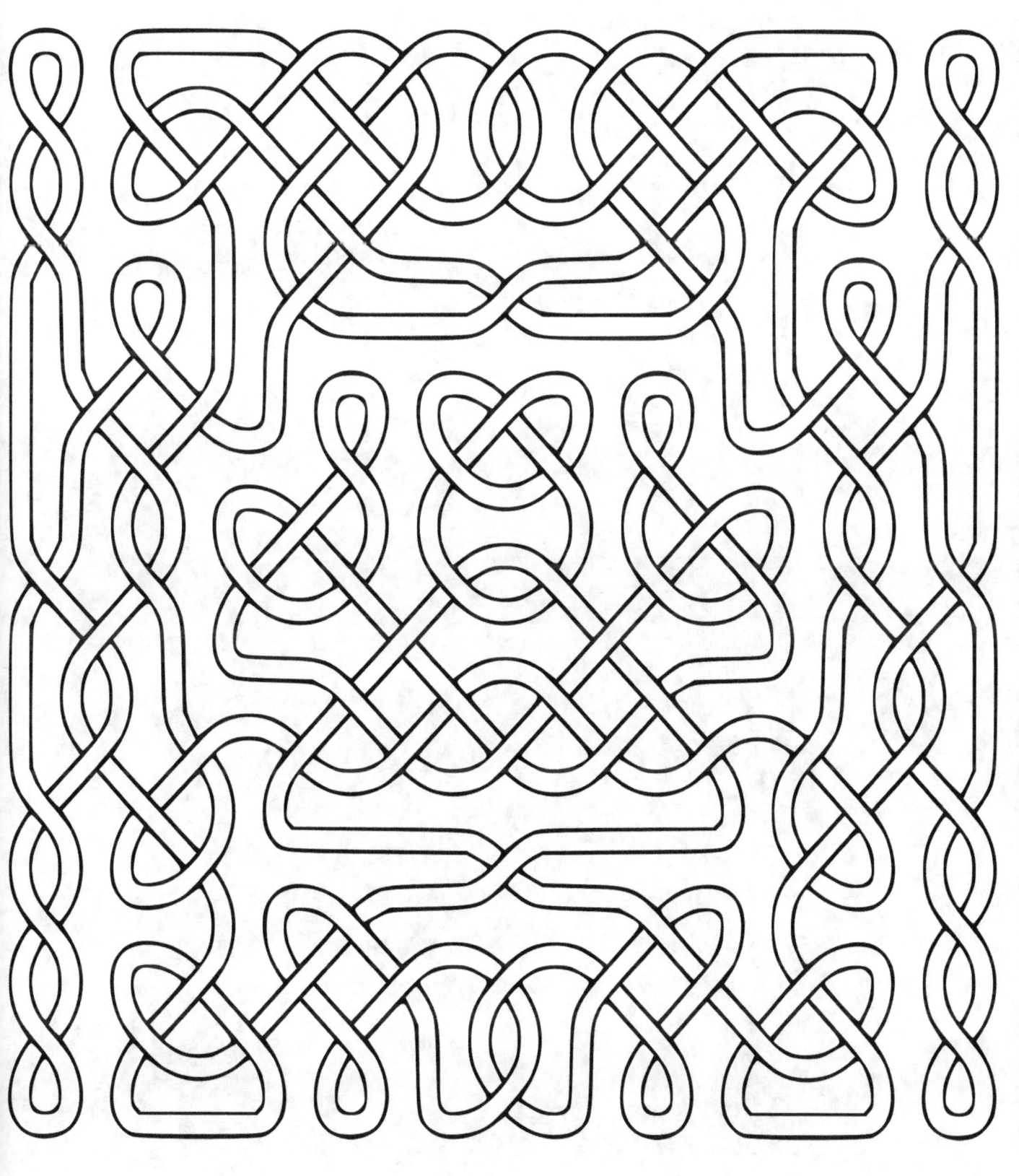

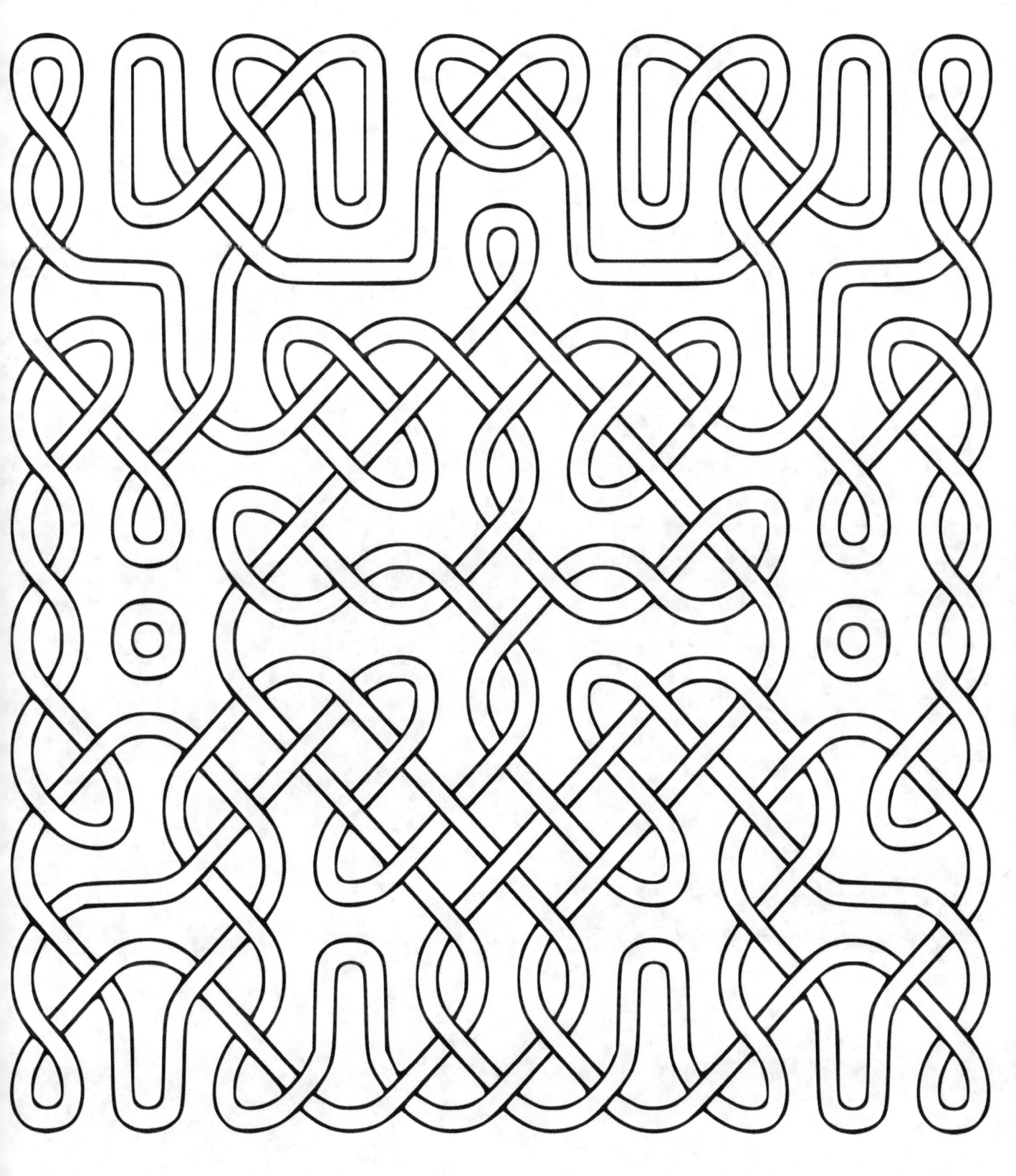

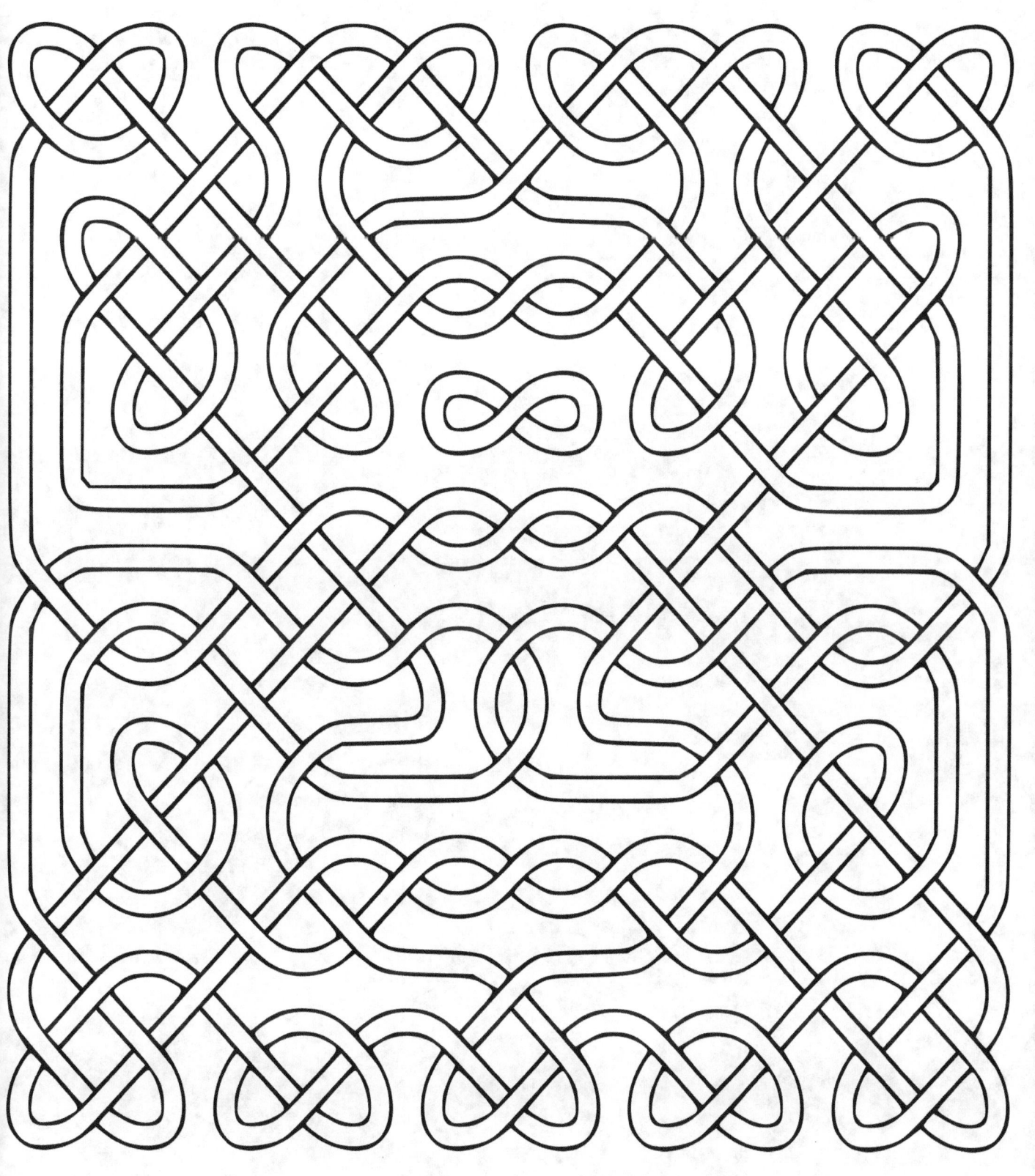

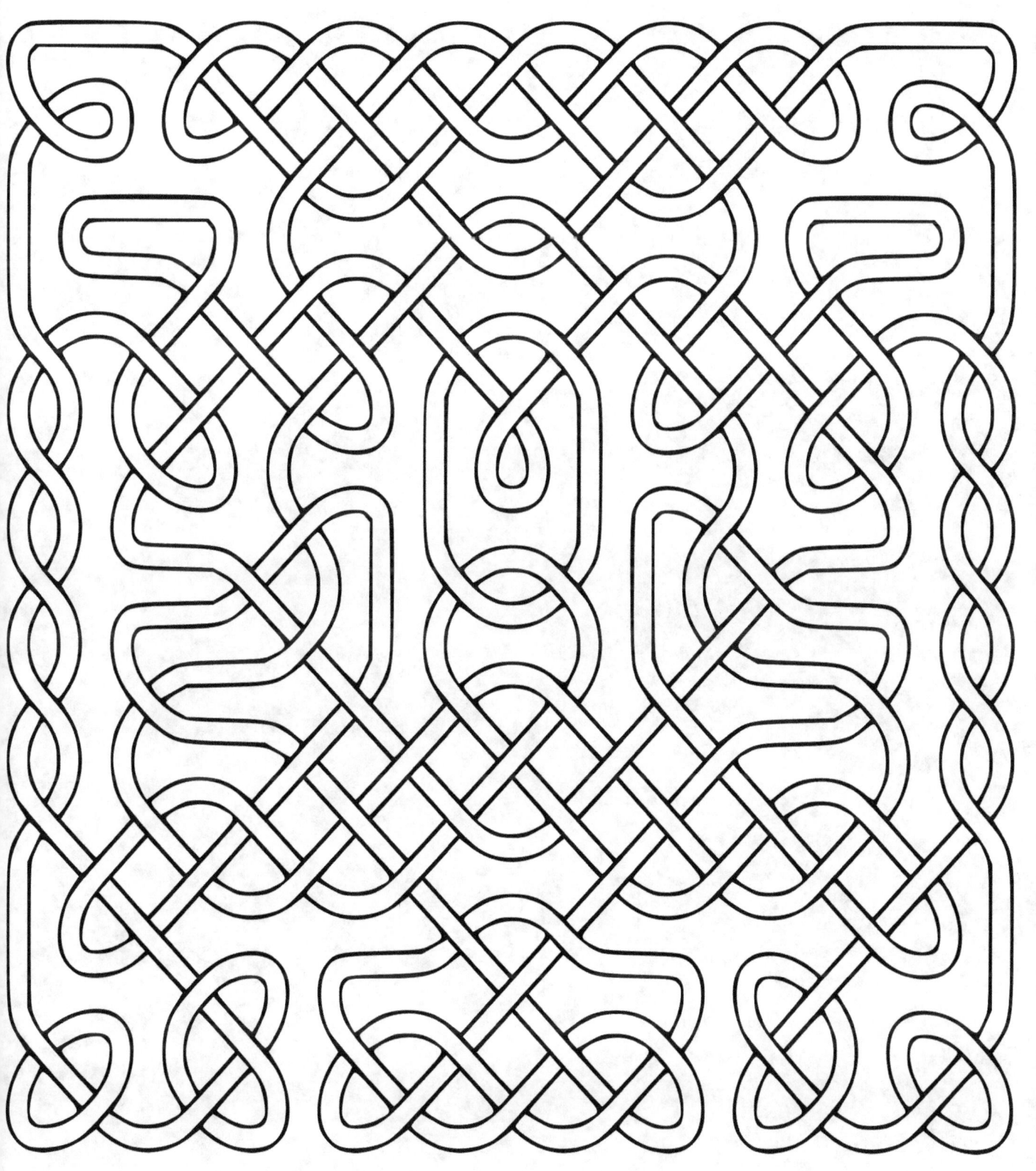

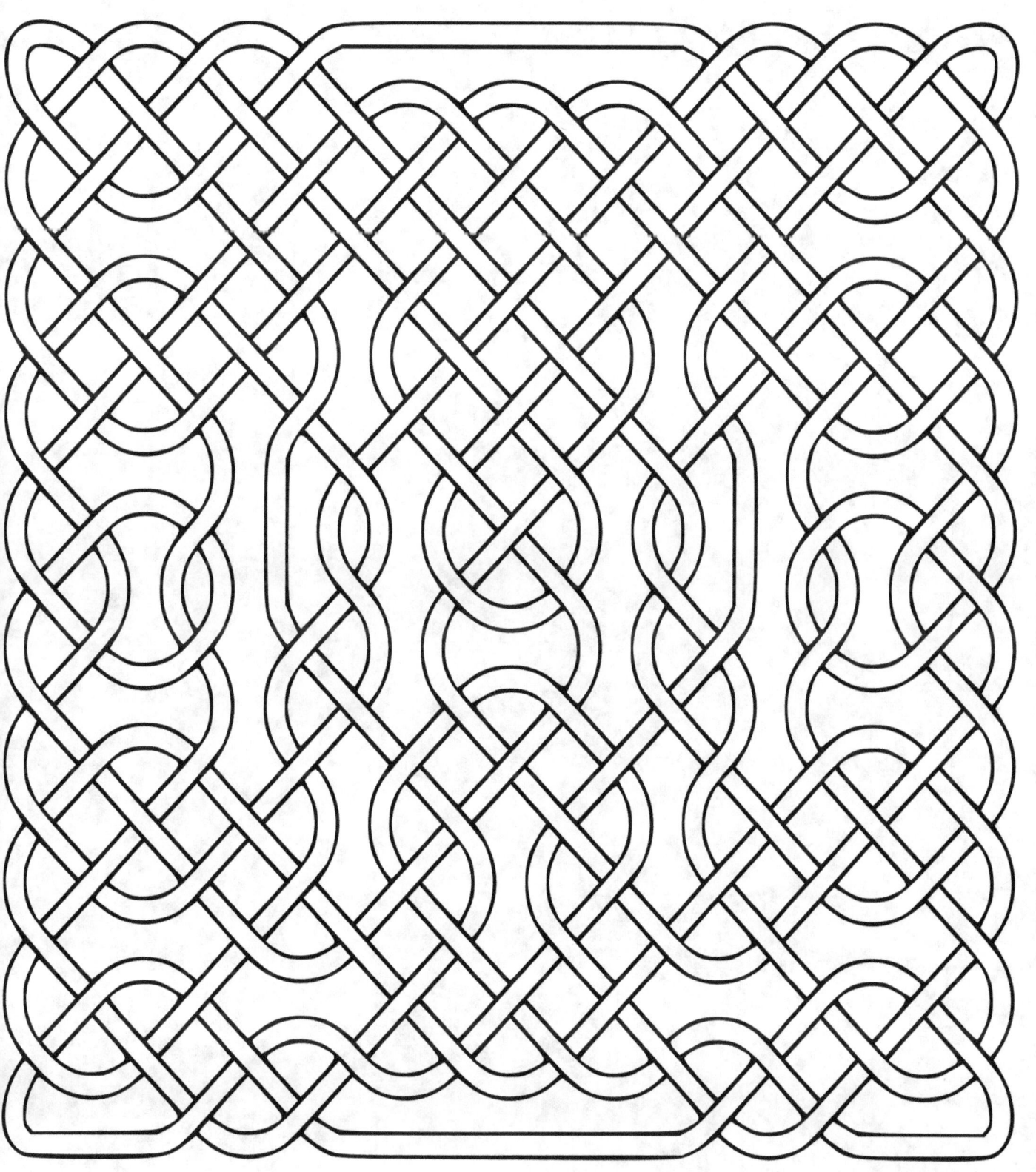

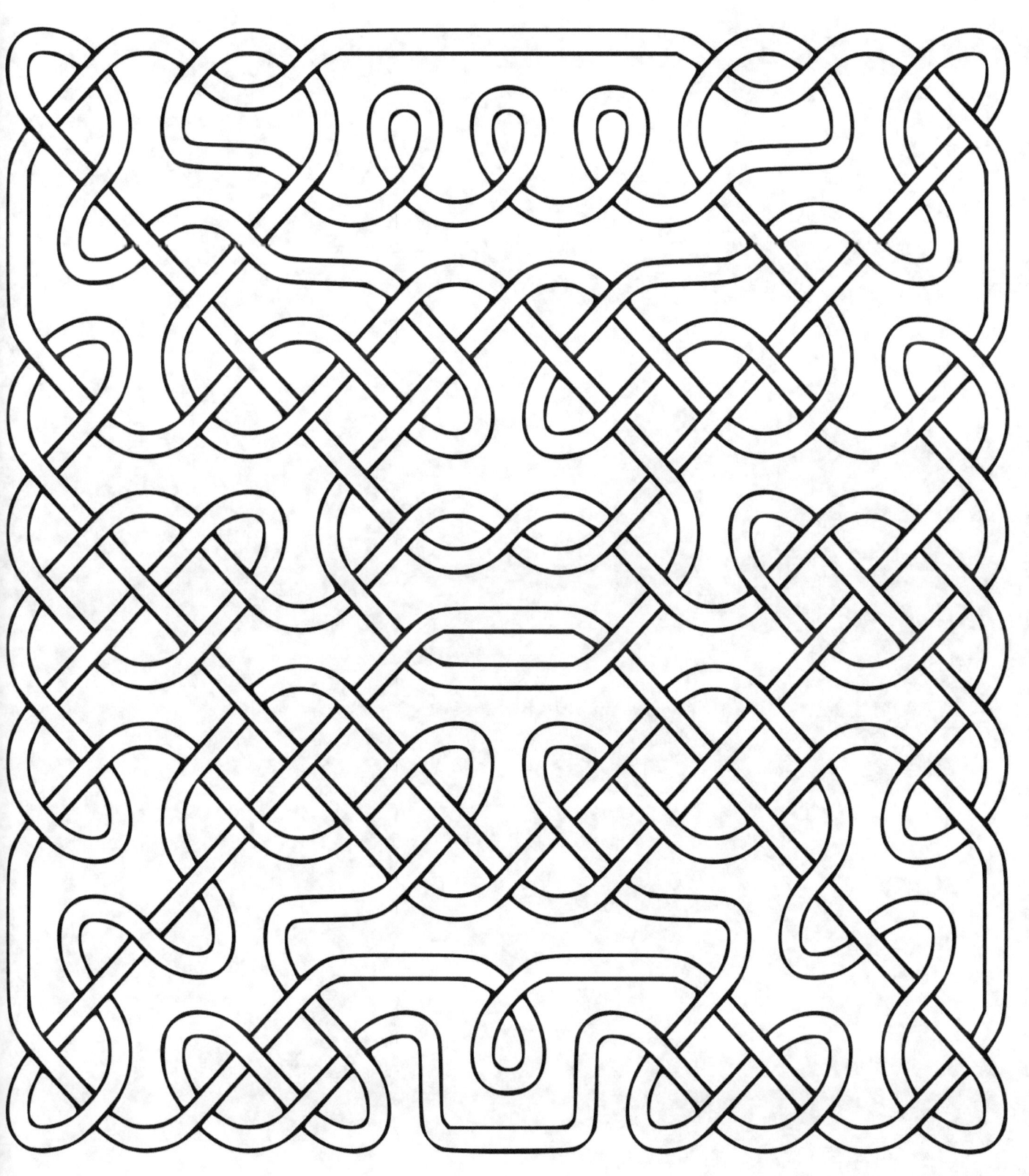

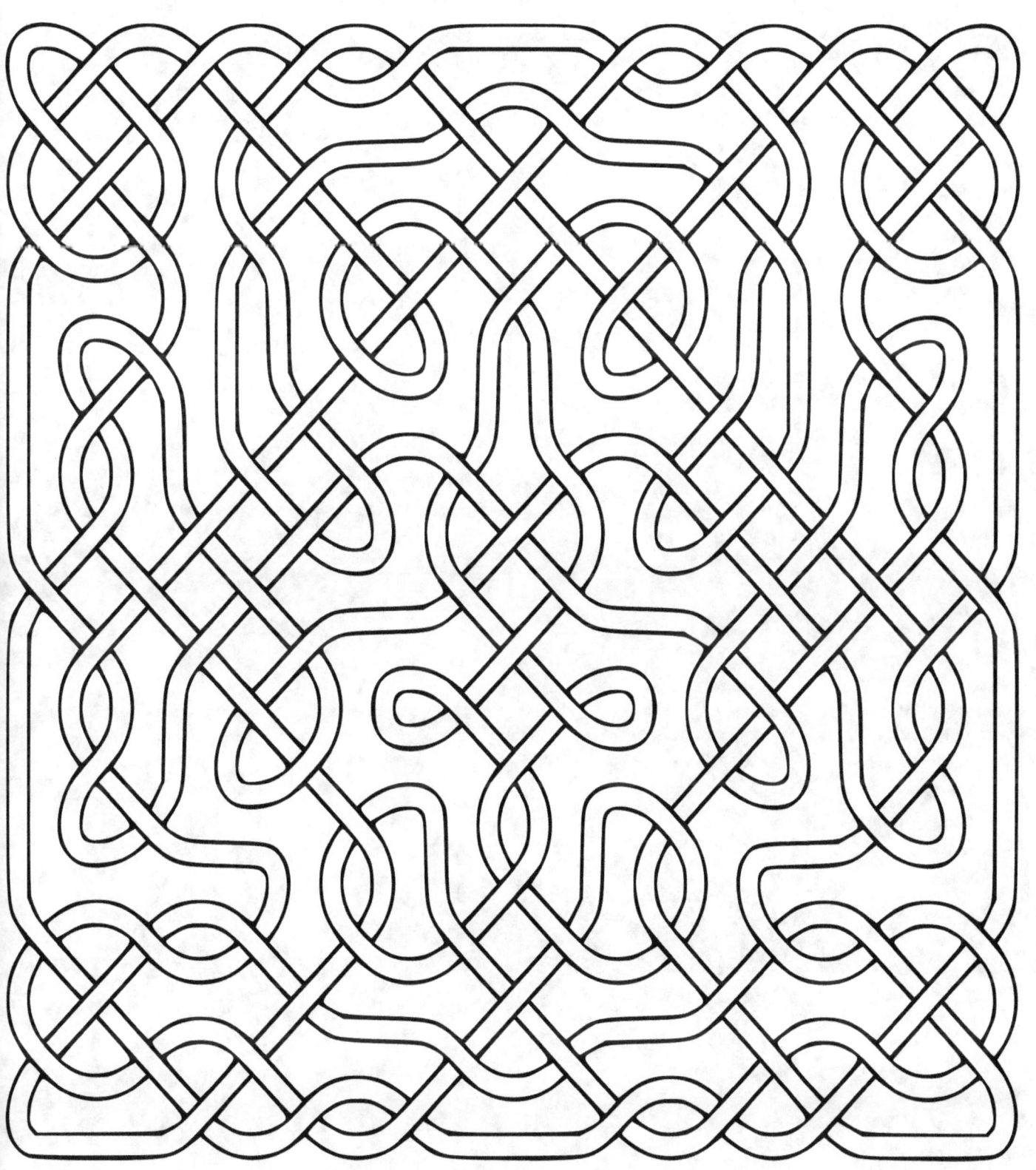

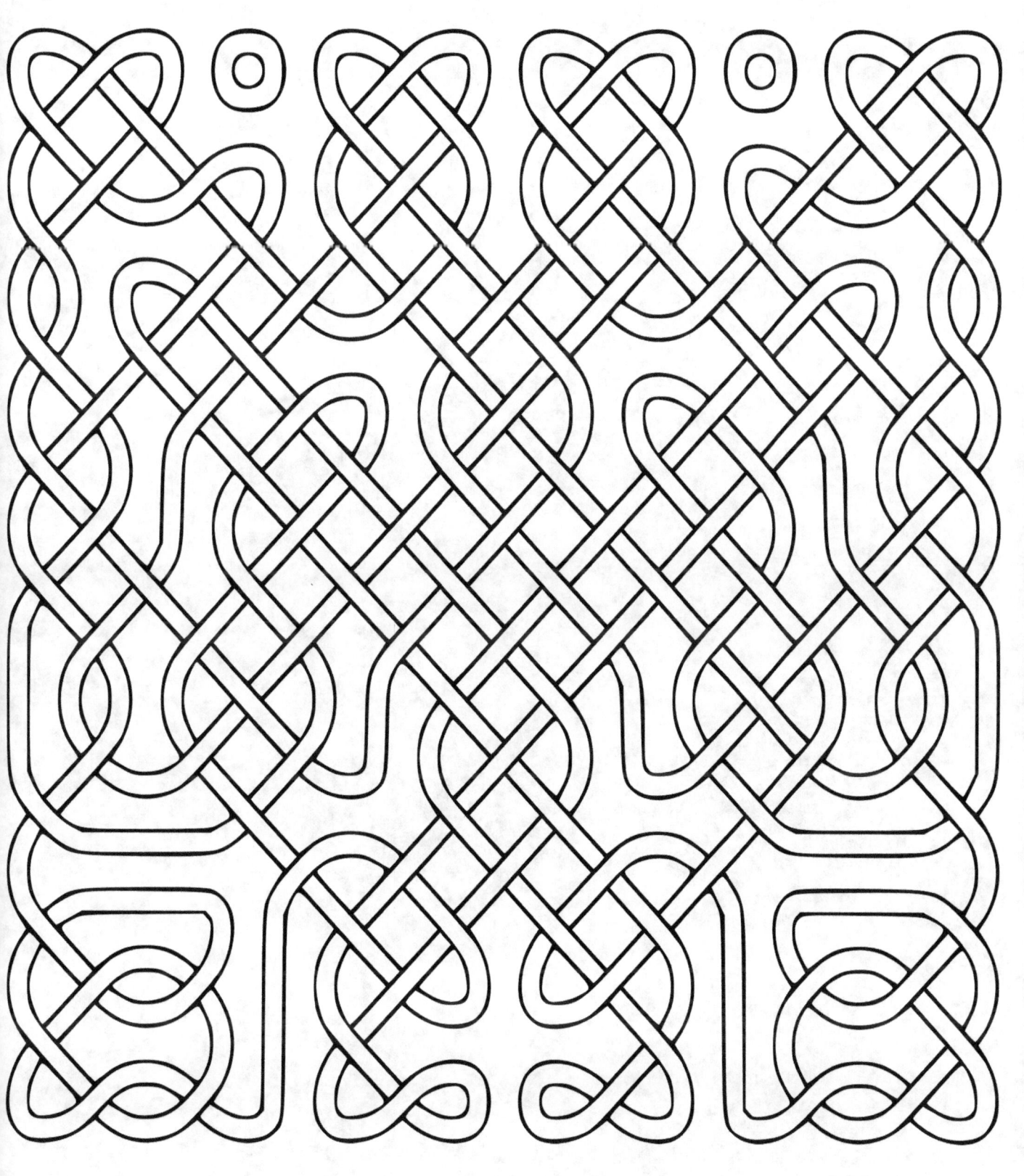

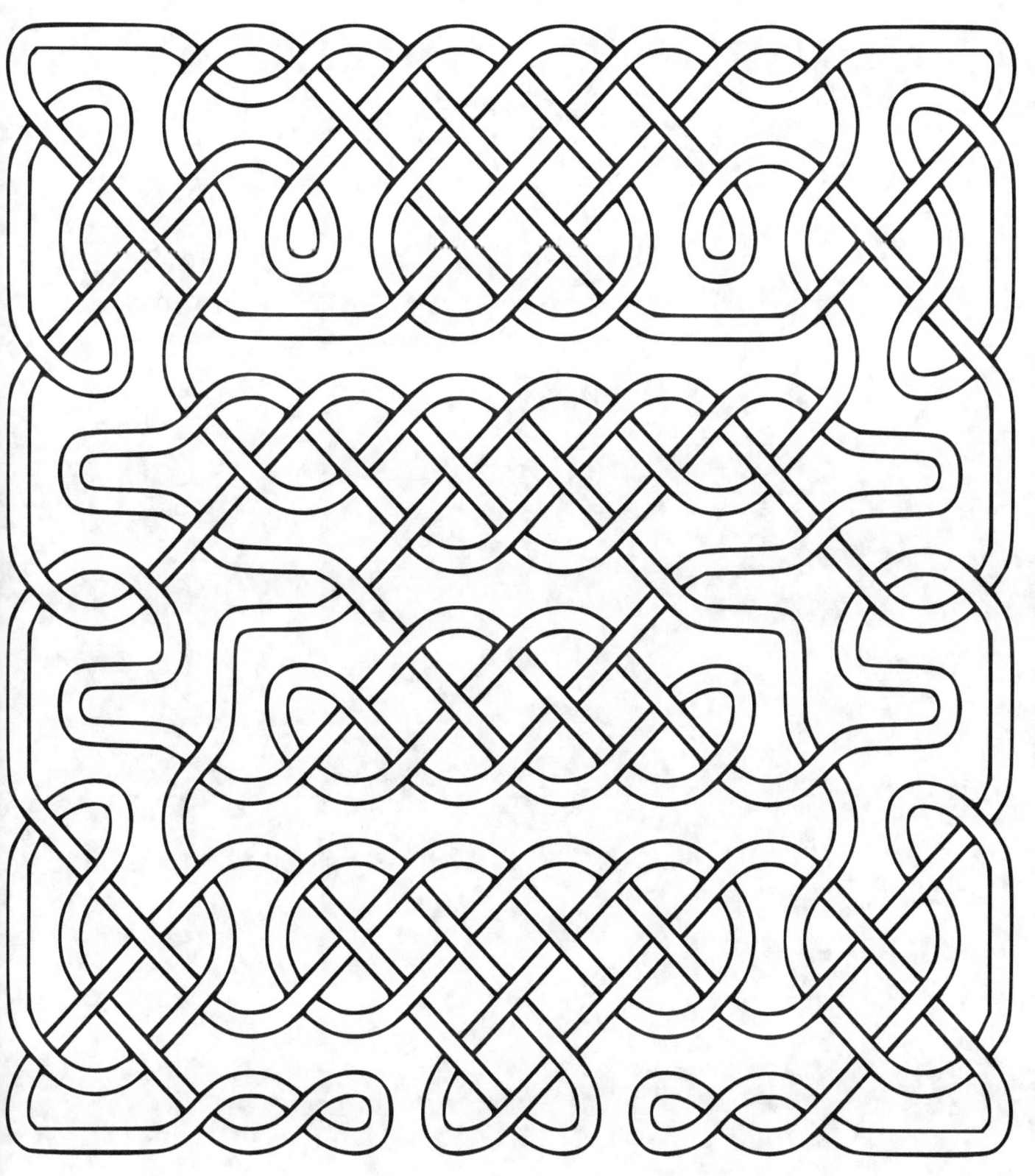

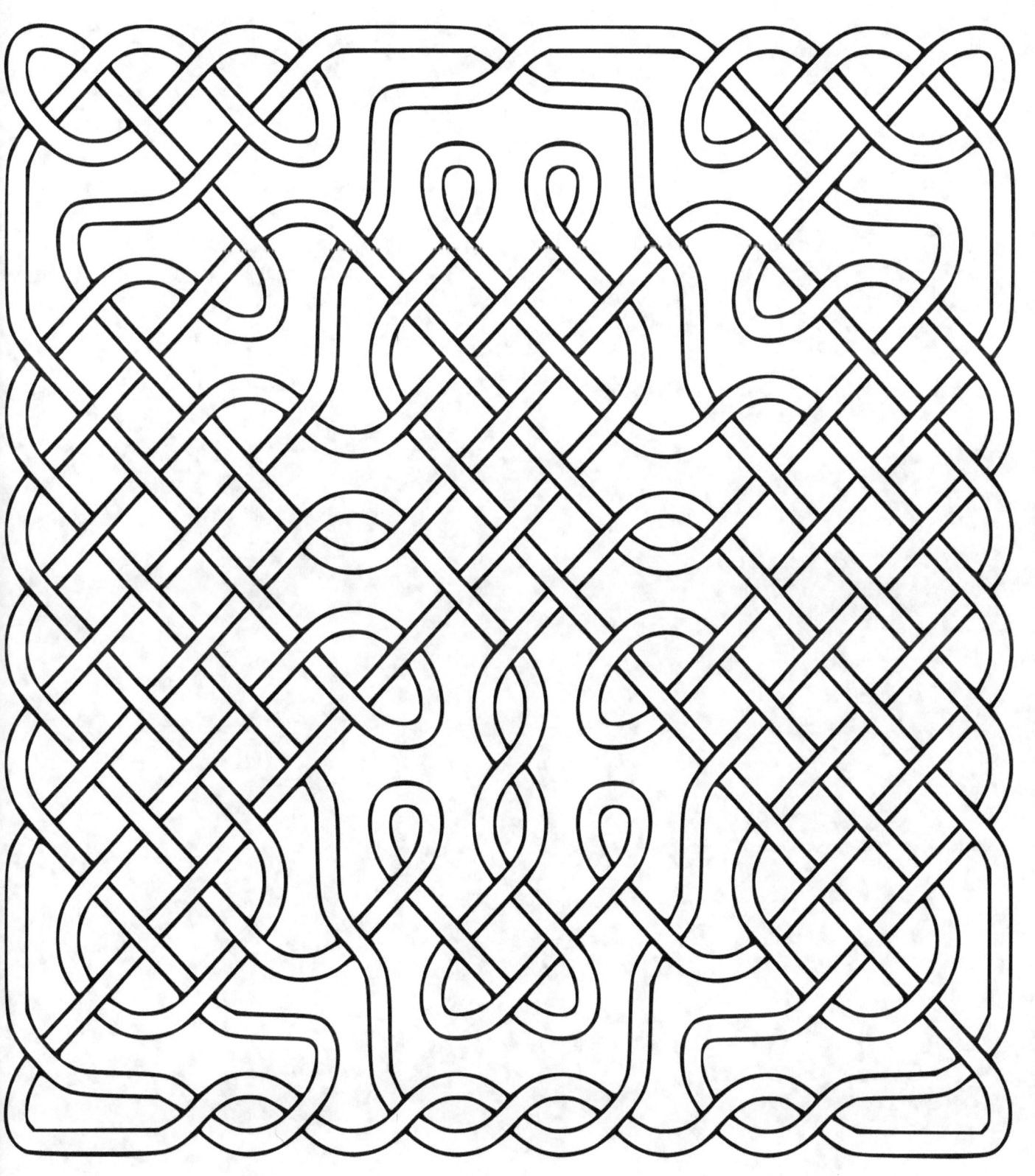

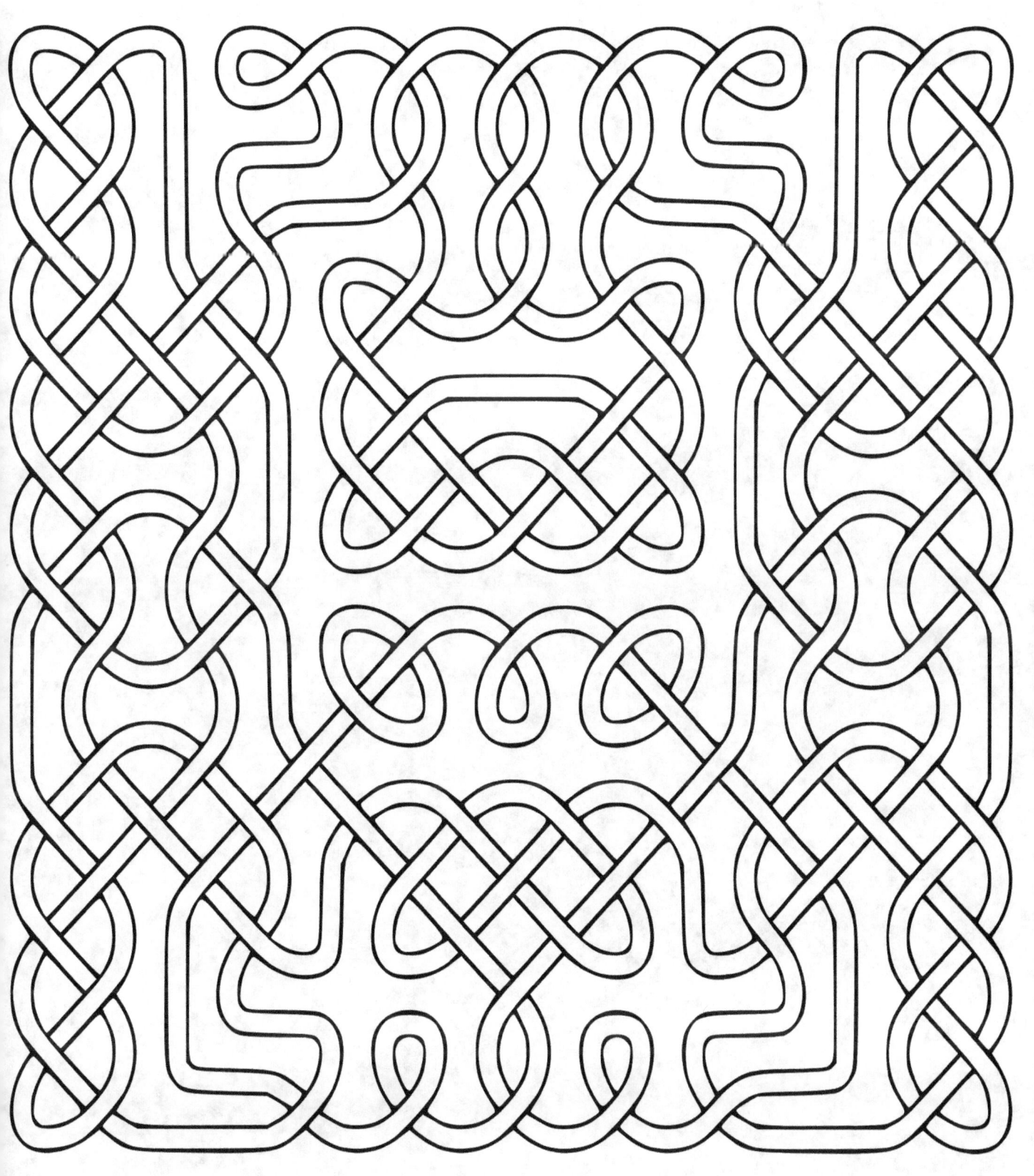

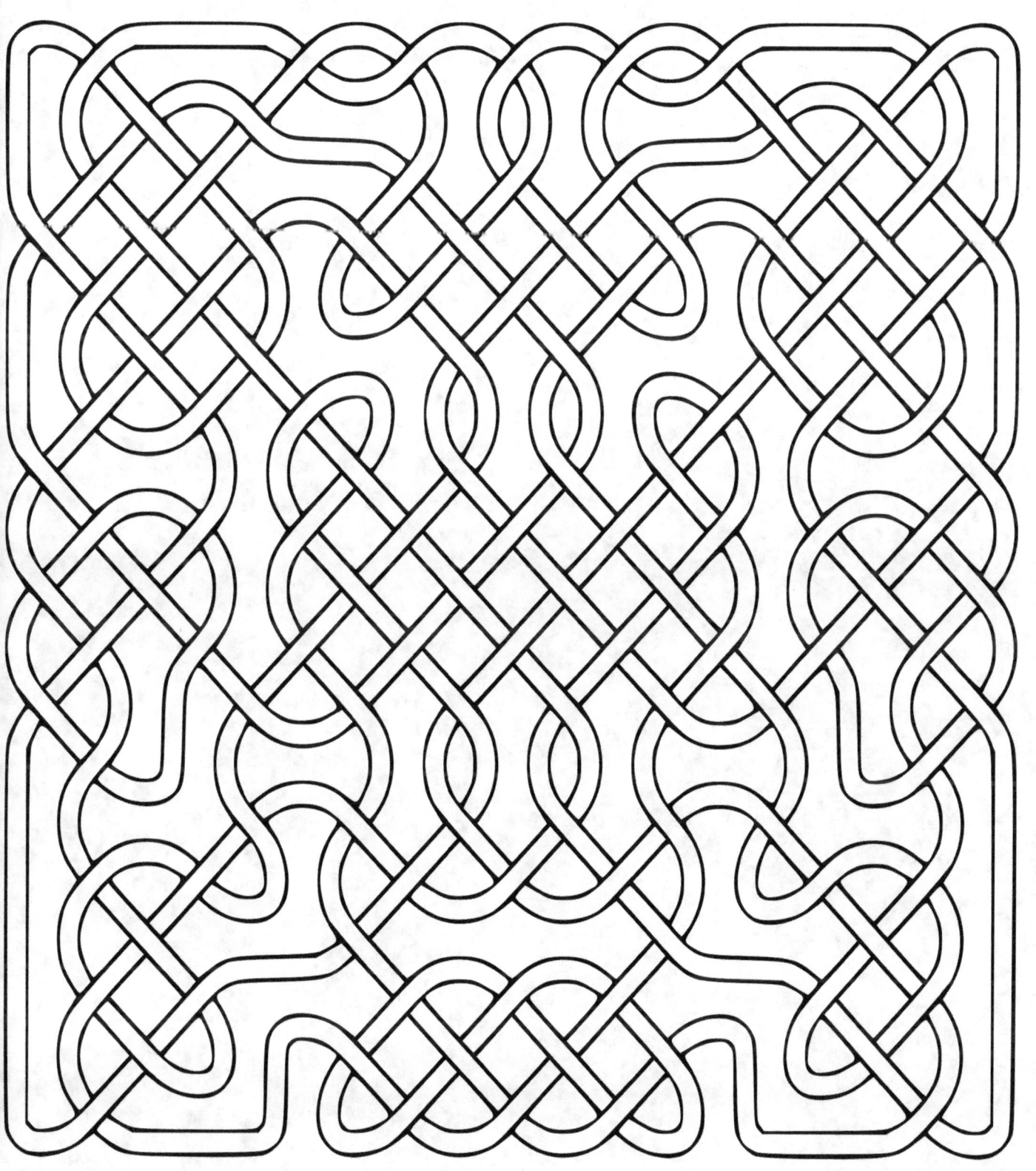

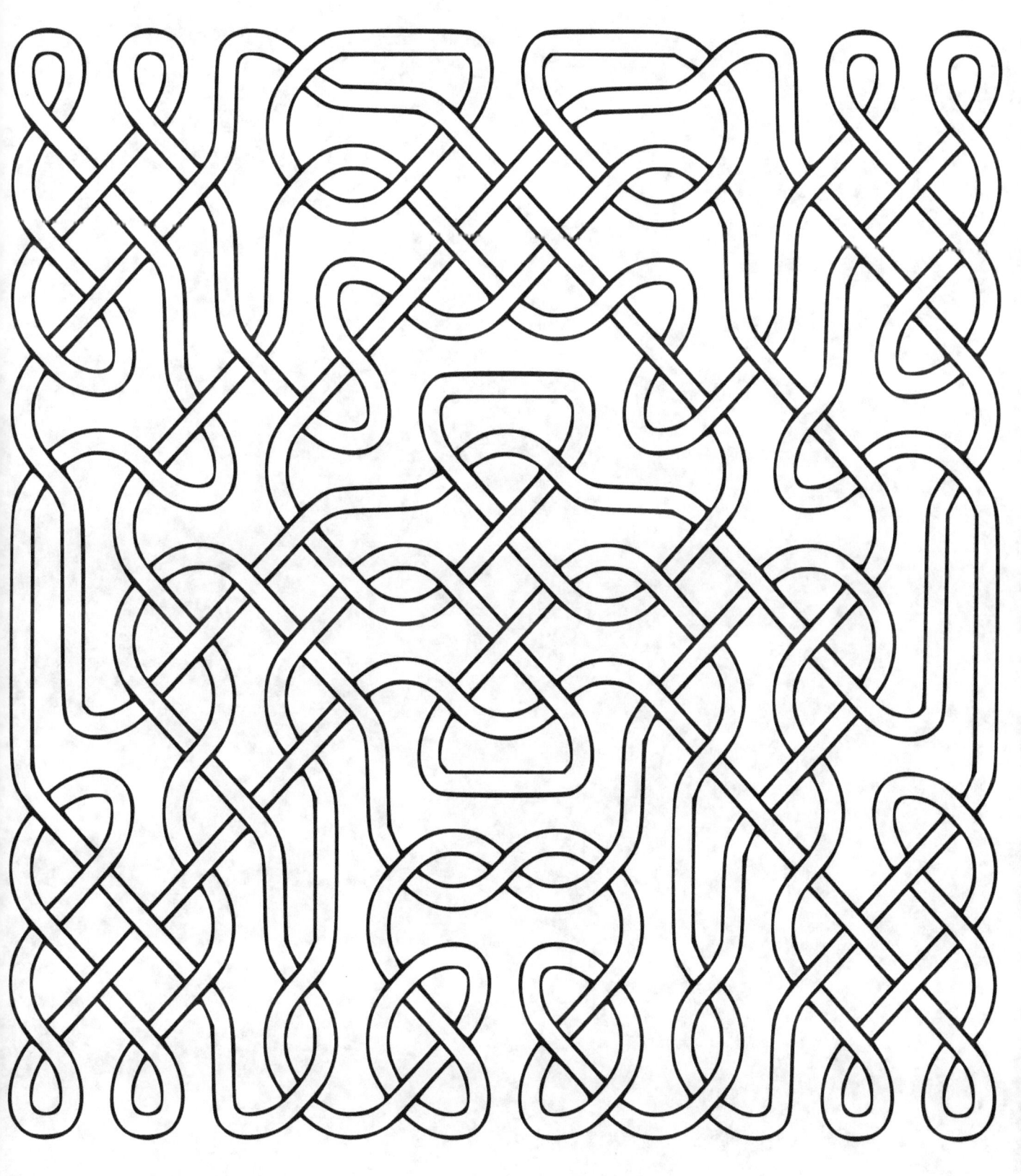

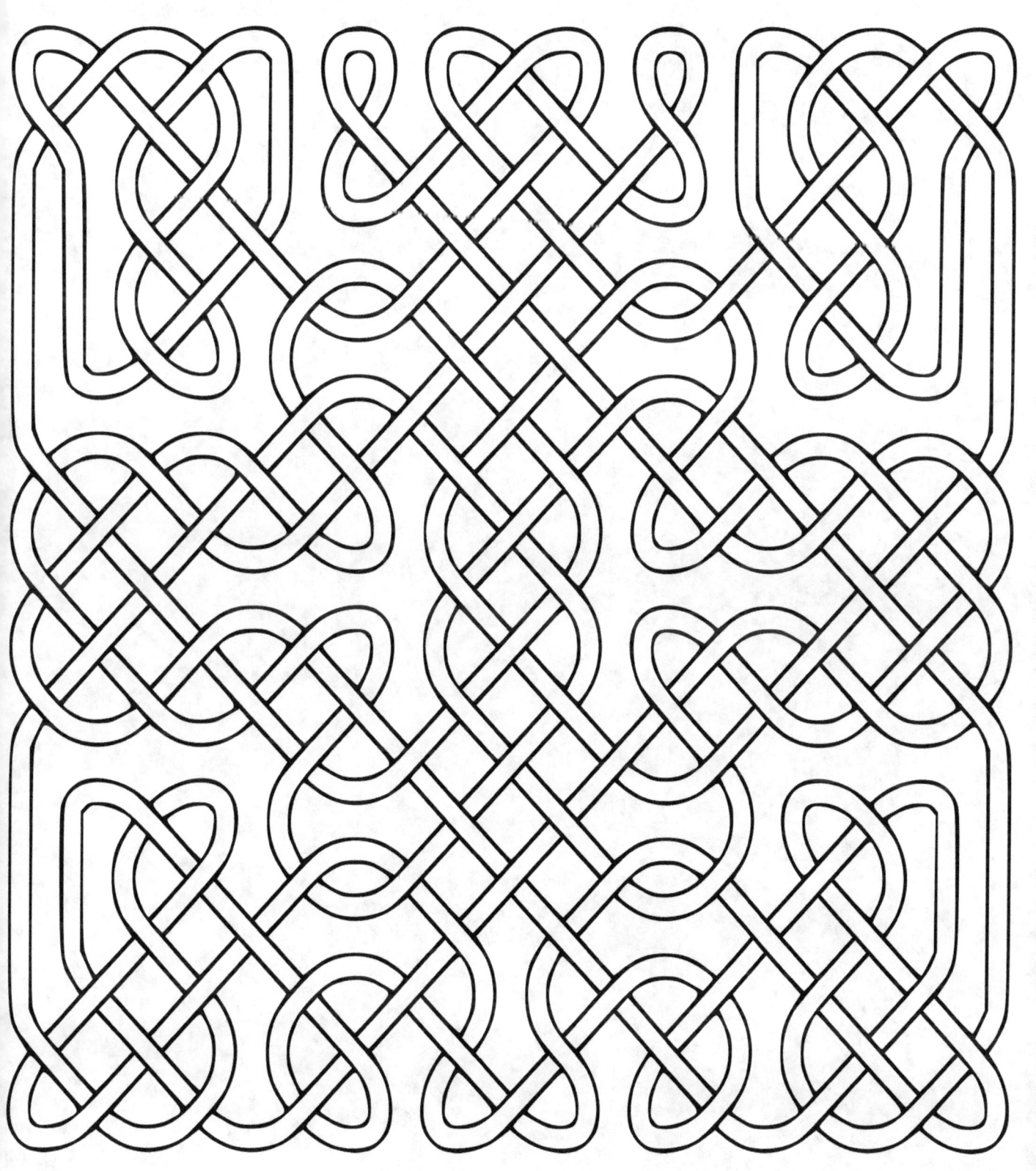

# ABOUT THE AUTHOR

In-between enjoying the outdoors, G.O. Molloy likes to create books for children and adults that tickle the funny bone, intrigue the imagination and calm the soul.

To find other titles by him hop over to:

http://www.gomolloy.com


http://www.amazon.com/G.O.Molloy

www.ingramcontent.com/pod-product-compliance
Lightning Source LLC
Chambersburg PA
CBHW08082518O526
45168CB00006B/2580